CW00400637

# Branch
# Lines of
# Worcestershire

# Branch Lines of Worcestershire

COLIN G. MAGGS

ALAN SUTTON PUBLISHING LIMITED

First published in the United Kingdom in 1994
Alan Sutton Publishing Limited · Phoenix Mill · Stroud · Gloucestershire

First published in the United States in 1994
Alan Sutton Publishing Inc · 83 Washington Street · Dover · NH 03820

Copyright © Colin G. Maggs, 1994

All rights reserved. No part of this publication may be reproduced, stored in a retrieval system, or transmitted, in any form or by any  means, electronic, mechanical, photocopying, recording or otherwise, without the prior permission of the publishers and copyright holder.

British Library Cataloguing-in-Publication Data. A record for this book is available from the British Library.

ISBN 0–7509–0602–2

Library of Congress Cataloging-in-Publication data applied for.

*Jacket photographs. Front:* Ivatt Class 4MT 2–6–0 No. 43106 on the Severn Valley Railway at Bewdley. (21.10.76, Revd Alan Newman) *Back:* 57XX class 0–6–0 PT No. 3607 leaves the Halesowen Canal Basin branch with a train of pipes and approaches Halesowen. (31.5.66, G. Bannister)

*Endpapers. Front:* 16XX class 0–6–0 PT No. 1661 crosses Shrub Hill Road, Worcester, with a train of vans containing vinegar from Messrs Hill Evans works. The spark arresting cowl was fitted in 1955 when the engine was new, to enable it to work at the naval armament depot at Ditton Priors. The railway-type signal halts road traffic, the shunter holding a flag as an additional precaution. (21.4.61, Ellis James-Robertson) *Back:* No. 7819 *Hinton Manor* leaves Bewdley Tunnel with the 1118. (24.9.89, Hugh Ballantyne)

Typeset in 10/12 Palatino.
Typesetting and origination by
Alan Sutton Publishing Limited.
Printed and bound in Great Britain by
Butler & Tanner Ltd, Frome and London.

# Contents

TO DUDLEY    TO BIRMINGHAM

STOURBRIDGE TOWN
JUNCTION
HAGLEY
OLD HILL
HALESOWEN
HUNNINGTON
TO BIRMINGHAM

TO BRIDGNORTH

ARLEY
NORTHWOOD HALT
WYRE FOREST
CLEOBURY MORTIMER
CHURCHILL &
BLAKEDOWN
KIDDERMINSTER
RUBERY
NORTHFIELD
LONGBRIDGE

BEWDLEY
BURLISH HALT
NEEN SOLLERS
STOURPORT
HARTLEBURY
BARNT GREEN
BLACKWELL
ALVECHURCH

NEWNHAM BRIDGE
CUTNALL GREEN
STOKE
WORKS
BROMSGROVE
REDDITCH

TO WOOFFERTON
DROITWICH
STOKE WORKS
JUNCTION
DROITWICH ROAD
STUDLEY & ASTWOOD BANK
COUGHTON
TO BEARLEY

FERNHILL
HEATH
DUNHAMPSTEAD
ALCESTER
WIXFORD

KNIGHTWICK
BROMYARD JUNCTION
SUCKLEY
YEARSETT
FOREGATE STREET
HENWICK
WORCESTER
BOUGHTON HALT
RUSHWICK HALT
SHRUB
HILL
SPETCHLEY
BROOM JUNCTION
SALFORD PRIORS
TO STRATFORD-
UPON-AVON

TO LEOMINSTER
STOULTON
PERSHORE
HARVINGTON
LONG MARSTON
BROAD MARSTON
HALT
PEBWORTH HALT

LEIGH COURT
BRANSFORD ROAD
NEWLAND HALT
NORTON
JUNCTION
ABBOTS WOOD
JUNCTION
WADBOROUGH
FLADBURY
HONEYBOURNE
TO OXFORD

MALVERN LINK
GREAT MALVERN
MALVERN &
TEWKESBURY JUNCTION
MALVERN WELLS
EVESHAM
BENGEWORTH
TO CHELTENHAM

COLWALL
DEFFORD
ECKINGTON
HINTON
ASHTON-UNDER-HILL

UPTON-ON-SEVERN
LODE SIDINGS
RIPPLE
BREDON
BECKFORD

TO HEREFORD
TEWKESBURY
ASHCHURCH

TO GLOUCESTER

0 1 2 3 4 5    10 MILES

## Key to all maps

| | |
|---|---|
| ——— | GREAT WESTERN RAILWAY |
| ⌒⌒⌒ | MIDLAND RAILWAY |
| ⊥⊥⊥ | STRATFORD-ON-AVON & MIDLAND |
| | JUNCTION RAILWAY |
| ┼┼┼ | GWR & MR JOINT |
| ○ | STATION OPEN 1994 |
| ● | STATION CLOSED 1994 |

# Introduction

The basic pattern of railways in Worcestershire was relatively simple. The Oxford, Worcester and Wolverhampton, known from its initials as the 'Old Worse & Worse', ran east to west across the southern half of Worcestershire and then turned north to bisect the county. Opened in 1853, the OWWR used some of its own standard gauge stock and hired the remainder from the London and North Western Railway. In 1860 the OWWR became part of the West Midland Railway and three years later was absorbed by the GWR.

The Midland Railway's main line ran through the county north to south approximately parallel with that of the OWWR. Although the MR owned a direct line between Stoke Works Junction and Abbots Wood Junction, quite a number of its trains used running powers over part of the OWWR to travel via Worcester. The MR also had a line from Barnt Green through Redditch, Alcester and Evesham to Ashchurch, which could be used as an alternative route to the main line as weight restrictions did not preclude the use of quite large engines.

Today the only former GWR branches which remain in BR use are those from Honeybourne to Long Marston, and Stourbridge Junction to Stourbridge Town, but the Severn Valley Railway flourishes in private hands. Although for most of its life the line from Droitwich to Lye and Birmingham was a main line, in recent years it has been relegated to secondary status and may be considered a branch. The only ex-Midland Railway branch still open is that from Barnt Green to Redditch, and with electrification in 1993 – the first in the county – its long-term future should be assured.

In order to have some logical sequence, the branch lines are described in order proceeding in a Down direction. Since Derby was the headquarters of the Midland Railway, this company considered trains travelling southwards to be Down. Paddington being the centre of the GWR empire, it followed that trains proceeding north through Worcestershire were Down.

As the county boundary has varied throughout the years, that chosen is as it was in steam days.

Grateful thanks are due to E.J.M. Hayward for checking and improving the text and captions.

# Barnt Green to Beckford

The first section of the Barnt Green to Beckford and Ashchurch branch was built by the Redditch Railway, an Act of 23 July 1858 allowing the raising of £35,000 in shares and £11,500 by loans. No time was wasted: the first sod was cut on 5 August that year and the completed line opened to passengers on 19 September 1859 and to goods on 1 October. It certainly benefited the community, one of the advantages it brought being that reduced transport costs caused the price of coal to fall by five per cent. On 1 October 1859 an excursion was run from Redditch to Birmingham Onion Fair for the very reasonable return fare of one shilling. An intermediate station at Alvechurch was opened on 1 November 1859.

Unfortunately the Redditch Railway ran into financial problems as its construction had cost £54,574 against an estimated sum of £35,000. Shares had only raised £27,120, which with the loan of £11,500 left a shortfall of almost £16,000. An Act of 7 August 1862 allowed the company to raise a further £15,000 by shares and loan of £5000, or powers to create debenture stock in lieu of loans.

Meanwhile, the Midland Railway Act of 7 June 1861 authorized a branch from Ashchurch to Evesham. This line was opened on 1 October 1864 with a procession of dignitaries to Evesham station, followed by a railway trip to Ashchurch. This branch did not entirely satisfy Evesham, which wanted a direct connection with the North. This was provided by the branch built under the Evesham and Redditch Railway Act of 13 July 1863 authorizing a capital of £140,000 in shares and £49,600 loans. The line was opened to Alcester for goods on 16 June 1866 and to passengers on 17 September the same year. The incomplete 380 yard-long tunnel under the southern part of Redditch prevented the line being opened right through to Redditch. The last portion of the tunnel was cut through on 1 August 1867 and the final section of the Barnt Green to Ashchurch line opened on 4 May 1868. On this date the original Redditch station was closed and a new one opened about a quarter of a mile to the south, close to the north portal of the tunnel. All three sections of the Barnt Green to Ashchurch line were worked by the MR, which eventually took over the Redditch Railway in January 1875 and the Evesham and Redditch Railway on 12 July 1882.

In the days before radio, television and telephones it was difficult to get the exact time, so from 12 June 1865 the guard of the 8.35 a.m. Barnt Green to Redditch and the 9.45 a.m. Ashchurch to Evesham was required to set his watch by the starting station clock and give the precise time to each station on the branch.

The line was very useful in providing an alternative route between Gloucester and Birmingham, avoiding the 2 miles of 1 in 37½ up the Lickey Incline. Throughout the year the line carried vegetables from the Vale of Evesham to London: early crops such as cabbages, Brussels sprouts and young onions in March, followed by asparagus until

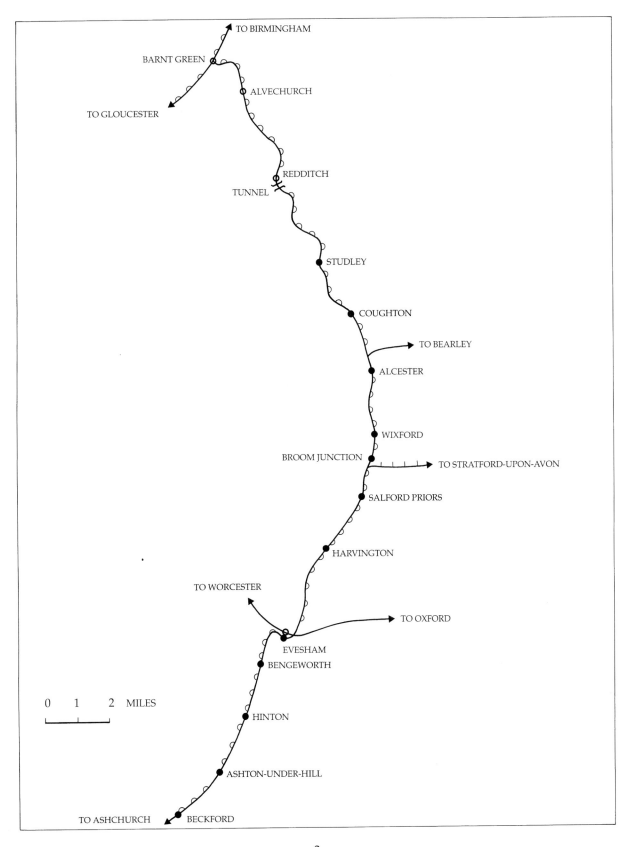

TO BIRMINGHAM

BARNT GREEN

ALVECHURCH

TO GLOUCESTER

REDDITCH

TUNNEL

STUDLEY

COUGHTON

TO BEARLEY

ALCESTER

WIXFORD

BROOM JUNCTION

TO STRATFORD-UPON-AVON

SALFORD PRIORS

HARVINGTON

TO WORCESTER

TO OXFORD

EVESHAM

BENGEWORTH

0    1    2    MILES

HINTON

ASHTON-UNDER-HILL

TO ASHCHURCH

BECKFORD

1282 class 2–4–0 No 176 at Barnt Green with an Up stopping passenger train. Notice the beautifully clean condition of the engine, including burnished buffers and smokebox door hinges.

*c.* 1910 Paul Strong collection

Rear view of EMU 310 103 at Barnt Green working the 0926 Saturdays–only Lichfield (Trent Valley) to Redditch. Its rear destination blind could be misleading. The train's state sadly contrasts with that of 2–4–0 No 176. The magnificent MR footbridge still stands.

5.2.94 Author

Burnt Green, view Up. The Gloucester to Birmingham main lines are on the left, with the Up platform in the distance. At the top of the signal ladder is a platform to stand on when changing the oil lamp and cleaning the coloured glasses. A newsboy stands near the base of the foot-bridge steps.

*c.* 1910 Author's collection

A Down HST driver's view of the junction at Barnt Green. A DMU to Redditch stands at the branch platform.

11.5.91 Author

June, which was strawberry time, and around 1904 30 tons of this crop were carried daily in June and July. In August and September the principal traffic was plums, 1000 tons being transported weekly. Autumn and winter saw the carriage of damsons, tomatoes, marrows, cucumbers, apples and pears.

In March 1958 the whole branch came under Western Region control and on 1 October 1962 the Alcester to Evesham section was declared by the engineer to be unsafe and was closed temporarily almost without warning. Midland Red buses connected Redditch with Evesham, calling at the intermediate stations, until 17 June 1963. The railway passenger service was never reinstated as, apart from Alcester and Evesham, less than 20 passengers used the stations daily. The line closed to goods on 13 June 1964. The Evesham to Ashchurch section closed entirely on 9 September 1963 because it was thought to be uneconomic to carry out the expensive track replacement required.

Although today trains for Redditch start from Lichfield, for most of the life of the branch trains originated from Birmingham (New Street). Barnt Green had two main-line and two branch platforms, the latter sharply curved. An attractive feature of the station is the MR foot-bridge spanning the four tracks. Today a waiting shelter is provided on the Down branch platform, but passengers on the Up branch platform have to share the Down main line accommodation; no shelter is located on the Up main platform. Beyond the platforms the branch line falls on a gradient of 1 in 75 and becomes single. The Worcester and Birmingham Canal is crossed on the approach to Alvechurch where the single platform and brick-built office is on the Down side. A new platform opened on 19 March 1993 was provided immediately on the Barnt Green side of the original. It is in a rural situation and has fields on either side.

Beyond Alvechurch the falling gradient continues to the trailing siding which led to Redditch gasworks. The line became double at Redditch North signal-box near the site of the first station. Before the advent of DMUs six locomotives were stabled at the adjacent one-road engine shed. Built of brick, it opened in 1872–3 and was a sub-shed of Saltley and later Bournville. In 1938–9 Redditch shed was re-roofed, the new structure being almost flat. Although DMUs from the Monument Lane depot began working to Redditch on 25 April 1960, the shed, sub to Bromsgrove since the branch was incorporated into the Western Region, remained open for two locomotives – either a 2-6-4T or 2-6-0 for one passenger train and also parcels working, with an ex-LMS class 3F 0-6-0T or ex-GWR 0-6-0PT as goods pilot. Following the closure of the shed on 1 June 1964 a diesel shunter was used. The goods yard was quite extensive, having a capacity of 188 wagons, excluding private sidings. An extremely large goods shed was provided for dealing with commodities manufactured locally such as needles, wire, fishing tackle, springs, batteries and bicycles. The yard closed to goods on 8 September 1969, but in the 1970s and early 1980s stone trains arrived at the yard behind a pair of class 24s, the stone being off-loaded into lorries for transit to road construction sites. Frequently all the sidings were full.

The two-road passenger station at the south end of the complex was built of brick. In 1972 this was replaced by a single platform with two faces sited a little nearer Barnt Green, but by September 1986 one-train working had been instituted between Barnt Green and Redditch so only one road was used. On 28 May 1993 the fourth Redditch station was opened. The platform has a single-storey, red-brick building and forms the terminus of the electrified Cross-City line. It is situated at the Midland Railway's 56¾ mile post, the distance being from Derby.

The line became single at Redditch South signal-box and one fireman remembers that during the Second World War the young signalwoman there when giving the single-line tablet came so close to the engine that footplate crews believed she would be struck, but she judged it correctly and was quite safe. South of the station the now-lifted line passed through a 380-yard long tunnel and just before Studley passed into Warwickshire, only to re-enter Worcestershire north of Harvington. The station there had a platform on the Up side with buildings of brick; the small goods yard had a 25 wagon capacity. The station closed entirely on 1 October 1962.

The branch rose at 1 in 137, crossed the GWR's Oxford to Worcester main line and became double before entering Evesham station adjacent to that of the GWR, both served by the same approach road. The temporary station opened on 1 July 1864 was replaced by a permanent one on 1 October. The substantial brick-built office block stood on the Up platform, but the Down platform lacked a shelter. In postwar years an economy was made by closing the booking office, passengers purchasing their tickets from the ex-GWR station. Near the Down passenger platform was a goods shed and a large fruit store. A junction with the GWR was opened by 23 January 1868. The 1960 Sectional Appendix to the Working Time Table warned that when transferring wagons between the former GWR and LMS lines, 'Before any vehicles are placed in this siding, or vehicles standing in the siding are set back towards the Worcester line, care must be taken to ascertain that vehicles are not being placed on the siding at the Worcester end'. It sounds as though this rule was prompted by a mishap.

Another local regulation read: 'Guards of trains brought to a stand on the Down line clear of the connection from the Up line to the Single line must immediately advise the Signalman at Evesham box that the train has arrived with the tail lamp attached'. This instruction was introduced due to the signal-box being sited at the south end of the passenger station and being in this position meant that the signalman could not see if a Down train was complete and had not blocked the signal line with uncoupled vehicles which could be struck by an Up train.

The goods depot was renamed Evesham South on 4 September 1951 and Evesham closed to passengers on 17 June 1963. South of the goods sidings was the two-road engine shed opened in 1870–1 and a sub-depot of Gloucester. Although closed on 14 September 1931, in 1954 engines were still stabled there.

The line between Evesham and Beckford was worked by telegraph bells prior to the introduction of the block telegraph system. West of Evesham the line, doubled to Ashchurch on 23 September 1890, crossed the Avon. Bengeworth, with a yard capacity of 24 wagons, closed to passengers and goods on 8 June 1953. As a wartime economy measure, single-line working was introduced between Bengeworth and Beckford on 31 January 1917, the Up platform being used at Ashton and the Down at Hinton. Double track was restored on 22 February 1921.

The line rose at 1 in 210 to Hinton which had a stone building, unstaffed from 31 August 1953. It closed to passengers on 17 June 1963 and the 32-wagon goods yard closed a fortnight later on 1 July. The summit was reached about midway between Hinton and Ashton under Hill and the line fell at 1 in 210/286 to Beckford. Ashton also had stone buildings and was unstaffed from 1 March 1957. The goods yard held 38 wagons and the station closed entirely on 17 June 1963. Its signal box had closed on 25 January 1910, when a ground frame was provided in lieu. Beckford ceased to deal with passengers on 17 June 1963 and goods on 1 July. James Taylor and Co. had a sizeable depot in the yard and supplied coal, coke and building materials over a large area. Fruit vans were despatched from the yard during the season. Beckford had a capacity of 78 wagons.

Not all trains on the newly electrified branch are electric. Class 116 Derby Suburban DMU T321 stands at Barnt Green with the 1024 Redditch to Lichfield (Trent Valley).

5.2.94 Author

The sharply-curved platforms at Barnt Green with the countryside beyond, are illustrated well in this photograph. A two-car Park Royal DMU is working the 1532 Birmingham (New Street) to Redditch.

19.9.64 Michael Mensing

A 2–4–0, probably No 104A, arrives at Alvechurch with an Up train. Notice the station-master's house, the brick-built station office and a supplementary one of timber but, in the interests of fire safety, with a brick chimney. There is an abundance of advertisements. Notice the barrels, cases, trunks and milk churns – the railway was an important carrier.

*c.* 1905 Author's collection

The original station at Alvechurch has now become redundant and been replaced by a structure immediately to the north. The station house is being demolished and the site of the timber-built office is occupied by a bus-stop-type shelter. The platform edge has been cut back. The view is looking towards Redditch.

5.2.94 Author

BR Standard class 4 4–6–0 No. 75060 arrives at Alvechurch with the 5.32 p.m. Birmingham (New Street) to Redditch, consisting of five coaches. This design of tender gave good shelter to the crew when the engine was working in reverse. Beyond the gate a cobbled path crosses the road. Notice the ribbon development along the road leading to the top of the station drive.

23.4.60 Michael Mensing

A three-car Suburban DMU leaves Alvechurch with the 1841 Redditch to Four Oaks. The goods yard was on the left. A platelayer's hut is almost swamped with undergrowth. This view shows the rural situation of the station.

15.7.78 Michael Mensing

The branch has seen quite a variety of locomotives. In the early days 2–4–0s and Kirtley and Johnson 0–4–4Ts worked passenger trains, with the occasional appearance of a 4–4–0. In 1907–8 Deeley 0–6–4Ts appeared and in 1934 four members of this class were shedded at Redditch. No. 2023 disgraced herself early in 1935 when she derailed at speed between Ashton under Hill and Beckford, and subsequently a 40 mph restriction was imposed on this stretch of line. Later tests proved that these engines were only suitable for working up to about 50 mph and above this speed riding was rough, oscillation and roll pronounced, and there was a tendency for the front end to develop an up and down surging movement. They did not enjoy longevity for the last member of this class was scrapped in 1938. The 0–6–4Ts were replaced by 2–6–2Ts and Fowler 2–6–4Ts. The four engines working from Redditch shed in the week ending 6 February 1954 were class 3P 2–6–2T No. 40117 and class 4–6–2T No. 42338, both of 21B Bournville; class 3F 0–6–0 No. 43599 and BR class 4 2–6–4T No 80063, both of 21A Saltley. Later, Ivatt class 4 2–6–0s appeared and in 1960 newer ex-LMS 2–6–4Ts with side-window cabs. On summer Saturdays in 1962, an ex-LMS class 3 0–6–0T worked a 57 mile round trip from Redditch to Ashchurch and back with four to six coaches.

Freight was generally handled by 0–6–0s, class 5 4–6–0s and class 8F 2–8–0s. In 1957 BR Standard class 9F 2–10–0s appeared on the Saltley to Westerleigh fitted freights.

With the closure of the Alcester to Evesham section in October 1962 severing the southern part of the branch from Redditch shed, as the branch had come under WR control from March 1958, WR locomotives from Cheltenham operated Ashchurch to Evesham trains.

Until 1913 banana specials worked from Avonmouth to London via the MR and Stratford-on-Avon and Midland Junction Railway, using the branch between Ashchurch and Broom Junction. The Barnt Green to Ashchurch line was valuable during both World Wars as an alternative route to the main line, also handling traffic from the London and North Eastern Railway via the former SMJR. On 4 June 1951 iron ore trains began operating from Woodford Halse and Banbury to South Wales, usually hauled by ex-WD 2–8–0s. Branch signal-boxes south of Broom Junction were kept open all night to handle this traffic, though in 1960 it was diverted at Stratford-upon-Avon to the former GWR line to Honeybourne and Cheltenham.

When the branch opened throughout from Barnt Green to Ashchurch the passenger service consisted of four trains each way and two on Sundays. By August 1887 four Down trains ran throughout and two in the Up direction, plus two more between Evesham and Barnt Green and seven more from Barnt Green to Redditch. By July 1922 the timetable showed three Down and two Up trains plus about nine short workings each way, while on Sundays two trains were run from Barnt Green to Evesham and back. July 1938 had a much better service: seven through trains each way plus about seven more from Barnt Green to Redditch. On Sundays five trains ran to and from Evesham, plus nine short workings to and from Redditch.

The introduction of DMUs on 25 April 1960 brought an hourly service to Redditch, though this was reduced to only two a day in 1964. However, the development of Redditch as a New Town with a population explosion from 25,000 to 65,000, saw the service increased dramatically. An average of 250 passenger journeys daily in 1978 rose to 650 in October 1980 and 1030 in November 1981, the line being boosted by the Redditch and Alvechurch Rail Users' Association founded in 1980. The publicity folder for the branch service in 1982 stated: 'If you have a valid rail ticket you can return from Birmingham on the Midland Red bus.' This information was amplified in the Redditch 'London Saver' leaflet: 'Upon arrival at Birmingham (New Street) after 1745 Mondays to

Ivatt class 4 2–6–0 No. 43013 (21A Saltley) leaves Alvechurch with the 4.25 p.m. Ashchurch to Birmingham (New Street). This photograph was taken on the last day of scheduled all-steam working on the branch north of Redditch.

23.4.60 Michael Mensing

The new platform at Alvechurch opened on 19 March 1993. Being almost straight it gives the guard a better view of boarding and alighting passengers, and is also nearer the road. View Up.

5.2.94 Author

This sign opposite the platform at Alvechurch prevents a stranger getting on a train going in the wrong direction.

5.2.94 Author

Saturdays [the last train to Redditch departed at 1748] passengers returning to Redditch may by surrendering their London Saver tickets at New Street booking office, obtain a ticket enabling them to return to Redditch by scheduled Midland Red bus service without extra charge. Passengers must satisfy themselves that a bus service is available and British Rail accept no responsibility for the suspension of bus services nor will any refund be allowed in this respect.'

An electric service was inaugurated to Redditch on 12 July 1993, but DMUs deputize for failures. Today there is a half-hourly service offering 35 Down and 34 Up trains on weekdays and 29 and 27 respectively on Sundays. In August 1887 the journey time from New Street to Redditch was about 55 minutes, compared with 41 today. Slight delays occur at Barnt Green when a Down train has to wait for an Up to clear the single track, or an Up train has to wait to move on to the main line.

Redditch: an Up train stands on the left as a Down train enters – its coaches will be well filled.

*c.* 1910 Author's collection

Ivatt class 2 2–6–0 No. 46492 leaving Redditch and going on the single line before entering the tunnel. It is working the 1.12 p.m. Birmingham (New Street) to Evesham on the last day of the Redditch to Evesham service.

29.9.62 Michael Mensing

Fowler class 4 2–6–4T No. 42383 (21A Saltley) calls at Redditch with the Sunday 8.10 a.m. Birmingham (New Street) to Evesham train.

30.3.58 Michael Mensing

Redditch: an 0–4–4T, probably No. 1250, has run round its Down train and awaits a path across to the Up platform after the Up stopping passenger train headed by a tender engine has cleared the section. Notice the very well-filled bunker on the 0–4–4T. The seven-coach train appears to be made up of five-compartment stock. A bookstall is on the left.

*c.* 1910 Author's collection

The terminus of the branch: left is the public convenience-style building opened on 28 May 1993. On the right beyond the stop blocks can be seen the 56 ¾ milepost.

5.2.94 Author

Ex-MR class 4F 0–6–0 No. 43975 (21A Saltley) drawing into Redditch station with an Up partly-fitted freight.

18.6.60 Michael Mensing

Plaque on the new station.

5.2.94 Author

Plaque on a catenary post, Redditch.

5.2.94 Author

This three-car Suburban DMU has arrived at Redditch with the 1204 from Four Oaks and will return as the 1340. This new two-platform station is on the site of the former goods yard.

14.4.79 Michael Mensing

EMU 308 134 has just arrived at Redditch with the 0753 Saturdays-only ex Lichfield (Trent Valley). The driver checks that the rear lamp is on before going to the other end.

5.2.94 Author

EMU 308 134, working the 0924 Redditch to Lichfield (Trent Valley), has come from the London, Tilbury and Southend line.

5.2.94 Author

Class 3F 0–6–0T No 47276 passes Redditch Up distant signal with the 1.15 p.m. from Ashchurch on the last day of passenger traffic.

29.9.62 Michael Mensing

2–4–0 No. 162 or 163 enters Harvington with an Up stopping passenger train. Notice the low fence, right, protecting the sloping station garden.

*c.* 1910 Author's collection

A general view of the MR station at Evesham. The goods sidings are on the right, a Down passenger train is at the platform and to the left is the carriage dock. Just off the picture to the left is the GWR.

*c.* 1910 Author's collection

An 0–6–0 leaving Evesham with an Up market produce special. The notice reads, 'LMS special train conveying 50 loads of market produce from Evesham to the North'. It stands by Evesham North signal-box, which closed on 20 January 1935.

*c.* 1934 Author's collection

Fowler class 4 2–6–4T No. 42421 (21A Saltley) crosses the ex-GWR line (a WR signal can be seen above the cab) and approaches Evesham station with the 5.10 p.m. Birmingham (New Street) to Ashchurch.

14.4.62 Michael Mensing

An Up strawberry special leaving Evesham behind 0–6–0 No. 3464 (7, Gloucester). In the foreground is the massive base of a water crane.

*c.* 1920 Lens of Sutton

Fowler class 4 2–6–4T No. 42416 at Evesham with the 4.30 p.m. Ashchurch to Redditch. The ex-GWR station can be seen beyond the tree.

14.4.62 Michael Mensing

Ivatt class 4 2–6–0 No. 43036 at Evesham heading an Up stopping train.

c. 1955 Lens of Sutton

Class 4P three-cylinder Compound 4–4–0 No. 40930 (22B Gloucester), pauses at Evesham with a Gloucestershire Railway Society special from Gloucester to the Cromford and High Peak Railway. At Derby No. 40930 was changed for a class 2P 4–4–0.

21.5.55 Hugh Ballantyne

Fowler class 4 2–6–4T No 42326 at Evesham with an Up stopping train. The Down train seems to be headed by a class 5 4–6–0. The station garden on the right looks attractive.

*c.* 1950 Lens of Sutton

90XX class 4–4–0 No. 9015 working the Railway Enthusiasts' Club 'The South Midlander'. It has arrived at Evesham in the Down direction.

24.4.55 M.E.J. Deane

57XX class 0–6–0PT No. 8743 at Evesham with the 6.47 p.m. to Ashchurch. On the right is the former LMS Railway's fruit store, then in use for storing chip baskets.

18.5.63 Michael Mensing

90XX class 4–4–0 No. 9015 leaves Evesham station working 'The South Midlander'. The ex-GWR goods shed is in the centre immediately behind the bridge.

24.4.55 M.E.J. Deane

57XX class 0–6–0PT No. 8743 at Evesham with the 12.24 p.m. to Ashchurch during the 'Big Freeze'.

12.1.63 E. Wilmshurst

Ivatt class 4 2–6–0 No. 43046 backing into a siding west of Evesham station after arriving with the 1.06 p.m. ex-Birmingham (New Street) and running round. The nearest trailer is loaded with vegetable crates, while beyond are hay-making rakes. The ex-GWR station can be seen beyond the crane.

14.4.62 Michael Mensing

A six-car Swindon Inter-City DMU at Evesham crossing from the ex-MR's Ashchurch line to the ex-GWR metals. The 9.00 a.m. Swansea to Birmingham (Snow Hill) used this route during the closure of the line through Broadway for extensive permanent way works. The former GWR engine shed is just to the right of the rear of the train and the flat-roofed signal-box opened only the previous year on 15 March 1957.

Sunday 30.3.58 Michael Mensing

A Swindon cross-country DMU working a Cardiff to Birmingham (Snow Hill) train crosses from the Ashchurch to Redditch line to the Worcester to Oxford line at Evesham when diverted during closure of the route via Broadway.

March 1958 P.Q. Treloar

Fowler class 4 2–6–4T No. 42416 arrives at Evesham with the 4.30 p.m. Ashchurch to Redditch. Above the brake van can be seen the former GWR engine shed, which closed in June 1961.

14.4.62 Michael Mensing

57XX class 0–6–0PT No. 3745 approaches Hinton with the branch's last passenger train, the 6.47 p.m. Evesham to Ashchurch.

15.6.63 Michael Mensing

The well-maintained garden at Bengeworth can be seen beyond the waiting shelter on the Down platform. A notice on the building reads, 'You may telephone from here'.

*c.* 1935 Lens of Sutton

57XX class 0–6–0PT No. 3745 leaves Hinton with the last Up train, the 4.30 p.m. Ashchurch to Evesham.

15.6.63 Michael Mensing

Three sets of three-car Swindon Cross-Country DMUs passing Hinton with the 9.00 a.m. Birmingham (Snow Hill) to Swansea service, diverted from the usual route via Broadway.

Sunday 30.3.58 Michael Mensing

Ashton-under-Hill, view Up. The red fire buckets hanging on the wall are labelled 'LMS', while on the opposite platform is a well-maintained garden.

*c.* 1935 Lens of Sutton

57XX class 0–6–0PT No. 3745 calls at Beckford with the branch's last passenger train, the 6.47 p.m. Evesham to Ashchurch. The 'B' headlamp is in the upper position on the bunker.

15.6.63 Michael Mensing

A Down stopping passenger train arrives at Beckford.

*c.* 1910 Author's collection

2000 class 0–6–4T No. 2024 leaves Beckford with a five-coach Up train. This engine was withdrawn in June 1937.

23.7.34 Lens of Sutton

Ivatt class 4 2–6–0 No. 43013 (21A Saltley) arrives at Beckford with the 4.25 p.m. Ashchurch to Birmingham (New Street).

20.2.60 Michael Mensing

57XX class 0–6–0PT No. 8743 at Beckford with the 12.24 p.m. from Evesham. Note the lower 'B' headlamp position.

12.1.63 E. Wilmshurst

# Great Malvern to Ripple

The Great Malvern to Ripple section of the Ashchurch to Great Malvern branch was built by the Tewkesbury and Malvern Railway, which received its Act on 25 May 1860 to raise a capital of £145,000 in shares and £48,000 in loans. Construction started from the West Midland Railway at Malvern and Tewkesbury Junction and the line opened to Malvern Wells on 1 July 1862, worked temporarily by the West Midland Railway, as the Midland Railway, which was to operate the branch, had no access until the line was completed through to Ashchurch. The line was opened throughout to passengers on 16 May 1864 but unusually for this period there was no opening ceremony. The occasion was not entirely overlooked, however, and early the following month the directors and friends celebrated by holding a banquet and ball at the Star and Garter Hotel, Richmond, Surrey. The fact that the celebration was so far from the railway whose opening they were celebrating was certainly most unusual, if not unique. The Tewkesbury and Malvern Railway was invested in the Midland Railway as from 1 July 1877. Most investors lost a considerable amount of money: only holders of first mortgages were paid in full. Holders of second mortgages received ten per cent, while Lloyds bonds and shareholders received just ten per cent also. The Midland Railway possessed running powers to Great Malvern and Malvern Link stations, though excursion traffic could only be worked to the latter. Branch trains were kept apart by the time interval system prior to the introduction of the block telegraph on 8 August 1890.

The section of line from Malvern and Tewkesbury Junction to Upton was closed to passengers on 1 December 1952 and the track between Malvern Wells and Upton lifted in September 1953. The passenger service between Upton and Ashchurch was withdrawn on 14 August 1961; the last train of two coaches, and thus double the normal length, was hauled by class 3F 0–6–0 No. 43754. The freight service was withdrawn from Upton and Ripple on 1 July 1963. The line between Malvern and Tewkesbury Junction and Malvern New Midland sidings was closed to goods traffic on 1 May 1968.

MR branch trains started from the splendid station at Great Malvern. Now Grade II listed, E.W. Elmslie designed not only the station but also its environs – the landscaped approach road and gardens, the roadbridge and Imperial Hotel, now Malvern Girls' College. When opened, it claimed to be the only hotel in England lit by incandescent gas. The single-storey station building was constructed of local stone – Malvern Rag. The clock turret and small spire were removed in the 1950s as Victorian monstrosities, but generally the station has been little altered. Quatrefoils are on the ridge tiles and the same decoration on the awning brackets. Each column supporting the platform canopy has on its capital different flowers and leaves, and in the early 1970s BR allowed a team of volunteers to repaint them in their former vivid colours.

The waiting room windows are unusual in having coloured glass. The station, partly destroyed by fire, was rebuilt and re-opened by Sir Robert Reid, BR chairman, on 20 May 1988. It is well worth a visit.

Another interesting and unusual feature is a special subway direct from the Down platform right into the adjacent hotel. At one time there was a siding at the Up end of the Down platform and via a wagon turntable trucks of coal were taken through a tunnel parallel with the pedestrian subway to the hotel, and later college, boiler room. This siding was taken out of use on 21 October 1956. At least until 1959 water for the college was supplied by the railway from pumps in Malvern Tunnel.

MR trains generally used the bay at the southern end of the Down platform and travelled for half a mile along the main line towards Hereford before bearing south-west at Malvern and Tewkesbury Junction. Here a single-road engine shed was built in 1864, the gales of January 1866 blowing off its roof which was replaced by a local builder. In 1883 the shed was renewed in wood at a cost of £126. The branch engine shedded there was normally an 0–4–4T. Although the shed closed on 14 September 1931, the adjacent turntable remained in use. The nearby Malvern Sidings were re-named New Midland Sidings in 1946.

From Great Malvern the line fell at 1 in 81 to Malvern Wells, renamed Malvern, Hanley Road on 2 March 1951 to avoid confusion with Malvern Wells on the Hereford line. Hanley Road closed to both passenger and goods traffic on 1 December 1952. The descent continued at 1 in 75/80 to Upton, renamed Upton on Severn in April 1889. It had substantial buildings in red and yellow brick. As there were no run-round facilities for a train of any length, a tow rope was kept in the signal-box in order to allow an Up train to shunt, otherwise the engine would have had its exit blocked by wagons. Following the closure of the section to Malvern, it became the terminus of trains from Ashchurch.

Single-line working by pilotman was instituted on the Down line between Upton and Tewkesbury for the week ending 9 July 1913, wagons being stored on the Up line, but the double line was reinstated on 27 August 1913. Single-line working was re-introduced on 18 February 1914 and this mode of operation changed to pilot guard working on 23 February 1914, and working by train staff and ticket from 31 December 1916.

South of Upton was the 24 yard-long Berry End Viaduct and shortly before Lode Sidings the five-span, 145 yard-long River Severn Viaduct. The latter included a chain driven sliding section over the deepest channel to permit the passage of tall-masted sailing ships. Lode Sidings were brought into use on 2 May 1938 to serve an Air Ministry installation.

The buildings at Ripple were similar, though by no means identical, to those at Upton, one difference being that instead of a light glass canopy over the exit from the booking hall to the platform, the doorway and platform were sheltered by a heavy, protruding gable.

Passenger trains were worked principally by Johnson class 1P 0–4–4Ts, but some 0–6–0s appeared, while in the 1940s Fowler and Stanier class 3P 2–6–2Ts were used. The branch was the last home of Stanier class 2P 0–4–4Ts. In later years Ivatt class 2 2–6–0s and Fowler class 3F 0–6–0Ts operated passenger services, but the final trains consisted of a WR 0–6–0PT hauling a single coach.

An initial service provided four trains each way on weekdays and two on Sundays, but the latter were withdrawn at the end of October 1867. The five trains to Great Malvern in 1880 were reduced to four by 1887. A lunchtime train was added by 1938 but the service was back to four in 1947. By the summer of 1958 the service had declined to two between Upton and Ripple and one in the reverse direction, while on Saturdays an extra train ran each way. This service remained until withdrawal in 1961. In 1890 a through service was inaugurated of one train daily between Malvern and Cheltenham, while in 1902 a through coach was run to Bristol from the branch. The Cheltenham coach was still running in 1946, the single non-corridor trans vehicle often headed by a class 2P 4–4–0.

Although the branch itself was not itself the scene of a serious accident, when on 8 January 1929 a Bristol to Leeds express overran signals in fog and crashed into a goods train at Ashchurch, the Malvern branch was used as a diversionary route.

Each of the platform canopy supports at Great Malvern has a capital with a different decoration. Today these are picked out in colour.

7.5.87 Author

The *porte cochère* and buildings on the Up side, Great Malvern. Notice the ornate clock tower, ridge tiles and lamps. The gardens in the foreground were designed by the station's architect, E.W. Elmslie.

*c.* 1905 Author's collection

Canopy support No. 11 at Great Malvern.

7.5.87 Author

The attractive platforms at Great Malvern, view Up. Notice the trees close to both platforms. The card is postmarked 5.9.06.

c. 1905 Paul Strong collection

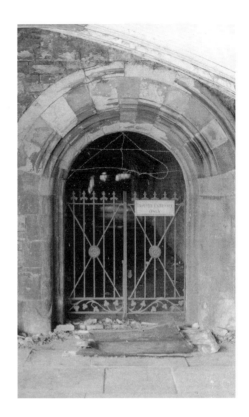

The private subway from the Down platform of
Great Malvern station to Malvern Girls' College.

7.5.87 Author

Restoration work, being carried out to the building on the Up platform following a fire at Great
Malvern station.

7.5.87 Author

A streamlined GWR diesel railcar of early design without drawgear and buffers, arriving at the Down platform, Great Malvern.

*c.* 1936 Lens of Sutton

An ex-LMS class 3F 0–6–0 standing at the Down bay platform, Great Malvern.

*c.* 1955 Lens of Sutton

Class 1P 0–4–4T No. 58051 at Upton-on-Severn with a train for Great Malvern. Notice that the signal arms for opposing directions are unusually on one post.

*c*. 1951 P.Q. Treloar

Stanier class 2P 0–4–4T No. 41900 at Upton-on-Severn with the 1.30 p.m. to Ashchurch. Notice the substantial station buildings relieved with light-coloured brick.

23.8.58 E. Wilmshurst

Class 3F 0–6–0 No. 43520, having arrived at Upton with the 5.10 p.m. ex-Ashchurch, is running round the coach to form the 5.45 p.m. return working.

6.6.59 Michael Mensing

44

A Great Malvern to Ashchurch train hauled by an 0–4–4T at Upton-on-Severn. Notice the attractive glass canopy and barge boards.

*c.* 1905 Lens of Sutton

Class 3F 0–6–0 No. 43520 sets back to couple up to the 5.45 p.m. to Ashchurch. Notice the goods shed behind the engine.

6.6.59 Michael Mensing

Ripple, view towards Upton. Notice the curved edge to the platform, the signal-box closed in 1910, and the fruit baskets piled on the platform and in the goods yard. The track dips under the bridge.

*c.* 1905 Author's collection

57XX class 0–6–0PT No. 4614 arriving at Ripple with the 5.45 p.m. Upton-on-Severn to Ashchurch. The engine draws a 'Pull and Push' coach and carries an incorrect 'B' headlamp.

29.7.61 Michael Mensing

A class 1P 0–4–4T shunts a goods train at Ripple. Notice the very heavy protruding roof forming a platform canopy.

*c.* 1952 Dr A.J.G. Dickens/Author's collection

57XX class 0–6–0PT No. 7723 with the 1.30 p.m. Upton-on-Severn to Ashchurch south of Ripple, crossing the M5 motorway under construction.

20.2.60 Michael Mensing

# The Halesowen Branch

The first railway to Halesowen was a branch from Old Hill to Halesowen authorized in a West Midland Railway Additional Works Act of 17 July 1862. It was intended that a junction would be made at Halesowen with the projected Halesowen and Bromsgrove Railway. Henry Lovatt won the contract and used ex-Cambrian Railways 0–6–0ST No. 18 *Cardigan*. The line between Old Hill and Halesowen opened on 1 March 1878. Although a branch to Halesowen Basin was included in the original Act, powers lapsed before it could be built and the branch was eventually constructed under the GWR Act of 2 August 1898 and opened on 2 April 1902.

On 5 July 1865 an Act of Parliament authorized the Halesowen and Bromsgrove Railway to build a line connecting those two places and also construct a branch to the Midland Railway at Longbridge. Two of the directors and several of its officers were common to the Harborne Railway. Financial difficulties arose and on 1 August 1870 parliamentary powers were given to abandon the proposed line to Bromsgrove. It was still intended to proceed with the line to Longbridge, but no contractor was willing to make the necessary financial outlay. On 13 July 1876 an Act changed the name of the project to the Halesowen Railway. Construction work started soon after this date and the completed works were inspected by the Board of Trade in August 1881 and, after modifications, were passed in May 1882.

Due to a dispute between the GWR, MR and Halesowen Railway over works the latter was supposed to construct at the MR's Northfield station, the single-track branch was not opened to passengers and goods, including Frankley public siding, until 10 September 1883. A celebratory public breakfast was held at the Shenstone Hotel on 1 October 1883. Under an agreement of 30 July 1872 the line was worked by the MR and GWR for 50 per cent of the gross receipts. In 1904 the company was declared bankrupt and following negotiations was vested jointly in the two companies on 1 July 1906.

Regular passenger services between Halesowen and Northfield were withdrawn in April 1919, and Old Hill to Halesowen was closed to passenger traffic on 5 December 1927, but workers' specials continued to use the branch platform at the Austin factory, Longbridge, for another forty years; a service from Old Hill to Longbridge was withdrawn on 1 September 1958 and New Street to Longbridge in January 1960. The line between Halesowen and Rubery closed completely on 6 January 1964, the last train being hauled by class 2MT 2–6–0 No. 46505 on 4 January. Rubery to Longbridge closed on 6 July 1974 and services were withdrawn on the Old Hill to Halesowen and the Halesowen Canal branches on 9 September 1968, though a traffic of ingots continued to run as required to Walter Somers Limited's premises opposite the goods shed.

From Rubery a standard gauge, single-line branch was brought into use in 1897 for contractor Abram Kellett's use when building Frankley Reservoir. This temporary line closed around July 1904 on completion of the contract. Kellett used six 0–6–0STs, three named after local places: *Rubery*, *Frankley* and *Northfield*. This line was relaid with 2 foot gauge track in 1924 to assist in the construction by E. Nuttall of Bartley Green Reservoir and was lifted in 1932. This narrow gauge line was worked by 17 four-wheel petrol-mechanical locomotives.

Another temporary branch was that built from a junction between Longbridge and Rubery to assist in the construction of Hollymoor Asylum. The half-mile-long standard gauge line was in place from 1901 to 1904 and worked by Manning Wardle 0–6–0ST *Hollymoor*, built in 1901.

The Halesowen branch left the Birmingham to Gloucester main line at Halesowen Junction immediately south of the present Longbridge station and climbed at 1 in 80 past the extensive sidings to the Austin factory to which lines were first laid in 1915 and subsequently increased. The branch entered Worcestershire just before Rubery, not far from where the Hollymoor Asylum branch made a trailing junction. Rubery, with a passing loop, had a brick-built station house with adjoining offices. The climb continued at 1 in 60 and then descended past Frankley Sidings, where the ground frame and sidings were removed on 13 October 1957. The line crossed the impressive 234 yard-long, nine-span steel trestle Dowery Dell Viaduct. This structure was only able to support the weight of smallish engines. It was dismantled in April 1965.

Hunnington had a single platform on the Down side, its brick building being similar to that on the Down platform at Rubery. The station closed to workmen on 1 September 1958. The yard had a goods shed, traffic including that for the Blue Bird Toffee works. The falling gradient of 1 in 50 continued to Halesowen. So far the branch stations were MR in character, but that at Halesowen was a GWR two-platformed affair, single storey in red brick. The passenger foot-bridge had stringers and landing supports made from old rails, timber planking preventing careless passengers from falling through the lattices. Until the opening of the line through to Rubery, Halesowen only had one platform situated on the west, Up, side of the line. Subsequent to the opening of the extension, a Down platform was added, but the track layout was such that any through Down train could not use it without reversing, though through Up trains could use the Up platform. By 1904 the layout had been further modified to allow through running to each platform, while a central siding was provided for stabling locomotives or rolling stock.

From Canal Basin Junction at the far end of the goods yard, the Halesowen Basin branch curved eastwards and then southwards, almost making a circle back towards Halesowen passenger station. En route it served the three sidings at Coombswood Colliery, which were lifted around September 1937. The basin, with its nest of more than a dozen sidings in addition to those used for transfer between rail and canal (covered accommodation was provided), had private sidings serving several industries.

Coombes Holloway Halt opened on 1 July 1905 with the introduction of steam railmotors. Its timber platform 150 feet long and 6 feet wide, with a corrugated iron pagoda, had a 1 in 5 inclined ramp giving access from Gorsby Road. In April 1913 the platform was moved from the east to the west side of the single line to allow the third side of a triangular junction to be built giving access to the canal basin. The new curve opened in 1914. This new junction was controlled by Halesowen Basin Junction signal-box situated immediately north of the halt. The halt closed on 5 December 1927 and the signal-box and new curve shut the same year.

The line climbed at 1 in 70 and became level through the 151 yard-long Haden Hill Tunnel, rising at 1 in 50 out of Worcestershire to Old Hill.

MR passenger trains usually consisted of an 0–4–4T and three coaches, two of which were six-wheelers. Most of the MR trains were 'mixed'. Until 1944 goods trains were worked by Kirtley double-framed 0–6–0s, but that year Johnson class 2F 0–6–0s were introduced, the latter sometimes stalling on the 1 in 50 bank to Frankley.

On 10 September 1883 the initial service was seven trains each way, four provided by the MR and three by the GWR. In August 1887 the GWR ran thirteen trains from Old Hill to Halesowen with one less in the reverse direction, trains taking 5 minutes for the journey. The service worked by the MR east of Halesowen was much less frequent, only five trains being run each way. They took 12 minutes to travel from Halesowen to Rubery and 15 minutes in the reverse direction. Although some steam railmotors were introduced in March 1905, the full service with twenty-one return trips on weekdays and thirteen on Sundays did not commence until 1 July 1905. The Divisional Superintendent at Birmingham wrote to the local staff on 27 June urging them to find an advertiser to take up the empty space on the reverse of the tickets sold by the conductors. The charge was £1 10s 0d per 10,000 tickets.

By April 1910 the steam railmotors working the Old Hill to Halesowen shuttle service provided twenty-seven trains each way, the MR still running five trains on its section. This latter service was reduced during the First World War and entirely withdrawn in April 1919. Until the Old Hill to Halesowen line closed to passengers on 5 December 1927, the railmotors made twenty-three trips each way. Unadvertised workmen's services ran until 31 March 1928. After the MR passenger services ceased in 1919, two through workmen's trains were run between Halesowen and Longbridge operated by GWR engines and crew. Until 1949 the WR used open-cab 17XX class 0–6–0PTs on these trains, but that year 74XX class 0–6–0PTs were introduced. Between Old Hill and Halesowen, and on the Basin branch, there were no serious weight restrictions and 57XX class 0–6–0PTs worked this section.

655 class 0–6–0PT No. 2718 crosses Dowery Dell Viaduct with a workmen's train to Longbridge comprised of clerestory stock. Notice the check rails designed to guide derailed stock onto the viaduct, rather than let it plunge down the embankment.

12.7.39 H.C. Casserley

Rubery station, seen centre left, from the quarry.

c. 1905 Author's collection

Rubery, view towards Hunnington: the Up platform is rather overgrown. Notice the MR pattern signal-box and the GWR home signal.

*c.* 1955 Lens of Sutton

655 class 0–6–0PT No. 2718, with an open-backed cab, crosses Dowery Dell Viaduct.

12.7.39 H.C. Casserley

Class 2F 0–6–0 No. 58261 coming off Dowery Dell Viaduct with a Halesowen to Longbridge train.

*c*. 1955 G. Bannister

Halesowen, view towards Rubery. Notice the station garden which won several prizes around 1910.

*c*. 1910 Author's collection

Hunnington, view towards Halesowen. Notice the goods shed on the right in the distance.

*c.* 1955 Lens of Sutton

GWR steam railmotor at Halesowen, with a locomotive-hauled train beyond.

*c.* 1910 Lens of Sutton

GWR steam railmotor at Halesowen, view towards Rubery. The driver is oiling the motion. Notice the signal-box on the platform, and the provision of a middle road to facilitate engines running round.

*c.* 1910 Lens of Sutton

## G.W.R.

## Halesowen

Luggage label.

## BECKFORD

Guards of passenger trains stopping at Beckford between 5.30 a.m. and 10.30 a.m. must perform the necessary attaching and detaching as required.

## REDDITCH NORTH BOX.

Engines in the engine shed and coal stage sidings must not foul the connection between the shed and the down main line without the permission of the signalman.

## STRATFORD-ON-AVON.

### Accommodation Crossing to Mr. J. H. Rowe's Farm, near Goods Shed:—

The Guards and shunters, or the driver in case of a light engine, must see that this crossing is kept clear, and that no vehicle or person is crossing or about to cross BEFORE any shunt is made over the crossing. The persons using this crossing have instructions when any horse-drawn vehicle is crossing the railway that the horse must be led, and the staff must see that this practice is strictly carried out and report immediately any case where it is not done.

### Messrs. Lucy & Nephew's Siding:—

Before a shunt is made from the Goods Shed sidings to this siding across the approach road, the guard or shunter must get the key to the padlock of the scotch block from the signal box, and must see that the crossing is clear before any movement is made with the engine or vehicles across the approach road. When the shunting is completed the scotch blocks must be placed across the railway and secured with the padlocks provided for the purpose, and the key returned to the signal box.

No shunt must be made in either direction across the approach road when a passenger train is due to arrive at or depart from the station.

### Public Footpath leading to Allotments and Racecourse:—

The guards and shunter must see that A CLEAR CROSSING is kept at this point, and that no one is crossing or about to cross the line BEFORE any shunt is made over the crossing.

## SHUNTING AT TOWCESTER STATION (Blakesley End).

A bell is fixed in a cupboard at the end of the centre girder of No. 12 bridge at the Blakesley end of Towcester Station and is connected with a bell in the Towcester signal box, for the use of guards and shunters to call the attention of the signalman to set the points as required to be used, in accordance with the code exhibited.

## HALESOWEN BRANCH (L.M.S. & G.W. JOINT).

Tokens, less than the usual length, are in use between Longbridge East and Rubery during the time the Longbridge West signal box is closd. When these tokens are in use up trains will run over the down main line between Longbridge West and Longbridge East, and the Longbridge West up and down home signals will be worked from Longbridge East signal box.

Trains between Rubery and Halesowen must not, under any circumstances, be worked by more than one engine each.

Should an engine fail on the Halesowen side of the large viaduct between Rubery and Hunnington, and it is necessary for such engine to be taken to the Halesowen Junction side of the viaduct, arrangements must be made for the engine to be worked specially, and six wagons must be placed between the train engine and the disabled engine in order that both engines may not be on any one span of the viaduct at the same time. A competent man belonging to the Loco. Department must, in all cases, ride upon the disabled engine, and a brake van in which a guard must ride, must be in the rear of the engine.

### Frankley Siding:—

Trains going towards Rubery having traffic to attach or detach at this siding, must be placed in the siding provided for the purpose, and the points in the main line must remain open for the siding during the time such trains are attaching or detaching traffic.

Extract from the LMS General Appendix to the Working Timetable, March 1937.

# Honeybourne to Long Marston

The Oxford, Worcester and Wolverhampton Railway's branch to Stratford-upon-Avon from the main line at Honeybourne was authorized by Parliament on 27 July 1846, but due to the difficult state of the money market, the single-track standard gauge branch was not completed and opened until 12 July 1859, intermediate stations being at Long Marston and Milcote. On 24 July 1861 the line was extended from its temporary terminus to the GWR's Hatton to Stratford branch, which resulted in through trains running between Leamington, Worcester and Malvern from 1 August 1861.

The GWR, which had taken over the OWWR, built a new line southwards from Honeybourne to Cheltenham and another north from Wilmcote to Tyseley, thus creating a new main line between Birmingham and Bristol. Doubling the branch from Honeybourne to Stratford was carried out by Messrs Walter Scott and Middleton, the Worcestershire section being completed on 28 April 1907. The branch became a main line when a service of express passenger trains began from Birmingham to Bristol on 1 July 1908, the fastest covering the distance of 98 miles in 2 hours 35 minutes. The only station on this line in Worcestershire was Broad Marston Halt, opened 17 October 1904 and closed on 14 July 1916. Pebworth Halt on the same site opened on 6 September 1937 and closed on 3 January 1966.

After the diversion of most inter-regional traffic by 8 November 1965, the line reverted to branch status, its only regular traffic being three freight and two parcels trains daily, following the withdrawal of the stopping passenger service on 3 January 1966. The line from Cheltenham to Honeybourne, and Long Marston to Stratford-upon-Avon was closed on 1 November 1976, leaving from Honeybourne to the Ministry of Defence depot at Long Marston as a long siding.

The junction station at Honeybourne has had quite a varied history. It opened on 4 June 1853 as a passing loop station on the single line from Oxford to Worcester. The track was then doubled either side of the loop on 20 March 1855, and with the opening of the Stratford-upon-Avon branch it became a junction on 12 July 1859. Its first station-master was Richard Bunn and he remained for over forty years, retiring in 1894 aged seventy.

Developing traffic on the Oxford to Worcester and the Birmingham to Cheltenham lines caused Honeybourne to become congested, so a new station was built in 1909. This had two platforms and a central island platform. The old station was lit by oil lamps, but the new was illuminated by acetylene gas. Wartime conditions, however, caused a shortage of carbide, so oil lights were re-introduced in 1917. Gas lighting was restored in 1928 and electricity used in 1942. Additional sidings were laid in 1924 to cope with the developing fruit traffic. Honeybourne closed to goods traffic on 1 June 1964 and to passengers on 4 May 1969. But this was not quite the end of the story, as the station was ceremonially re-opened on 22 May 1981 and to the public three days later.

The first engine shed at Honeybourne was a single-road, brick-built affair. Its site required for station improvements, it closed in 1907 and the 1909 replacement building burnt down on 13 September 1911. Never restored, engines remained in the open for fifty-four years until the depot closed in December 1965.

During the Second World War an infra-red lamp was set up in the centre of the triangular junction and used for bombing practice. This infra-red light marked film carried by a bomber and indicated whether the bomb would have been on target.

At first the branch was worked by tender engines, but from 1861 the line was worked by No. 68, later GWR No. 225, a Beyer, Peacock 2–4–0T. In the early 1880s 517 class 0–4–2Ts appeared. About 1905 steam railmotors took over some of the workings between Honeybourne and Stratford. In the later years of the GWR, the local services were covered by through Worcester and Evesham to Leamington or Birmingham workings handled by tender engines, 4–4–0 'Bulldogs' predominating until the early 1950s when they were replaced by 2251 class 0–6–0s, 43XX 2–6–0s, or more occasionally BR Standard class 2 2–6–0s.

In August 1887 five Up and four Down trains ran on the branch. By April 1910 the service had improved to eight stopping trains each way, while the service immediately before closure was thirteen each way.

Honeybourne, view Down. An 0–4–2T heads an auto train, while a Down train is being loaded at the opposite platform.

*c.* 1938 Lens of Sutton

An Up stopping train comprising two clerestory coaches approaches Honeybourne. Notice the water cranes and loading gauge.

1938 P.J. Garland

Honeybourne, view Up. A train of four coaches hauled by a tender engine.

*c.* 1905 Author's collection

A busy scene at Honeybourne Junction, with three trains visible. The nearest milk churns are labelled 'Dairy Supply'. The view is taken in the Up direction.

*c.* 1910 Author's collection

The 2.30 p.m. from Cheltenham, comprising an auto car and an 0–4–2T, stands at Honeybourne Junction Down island platform.

27.2.60 E. Wilmshurst

43XX No. 6345, heading an Up goods, being watered at Honeybourne Junction and in all probability awaiting the assistance of a banking engine at the rear.

c. 1963 P.J. Garland

An Oxford to Worcester train drawn by a 2–4–0 passes at Honeybourne West Loop the construction works of the Cheltenham to Honeybourne line. A contractor's 0–6–0ST is on the left.

1903 Author's collection

A six-car Swindon Inter-City DMU working the 12.25 p.m. Birmingham (Snow Hill) to Cardiff (General) takes the north to west curve at Honeybourne to travel via Evesham and Ashchurch, due to closure of the Honeybourne to Broadway and Cheltenham route for extensive permanent way works.

23.9.57 Michael Mensing

Intending passengers at Pebworth Halt faced a steep climb.

March 1967 D.J. Hyde

Pebworth Halt, view Up. The concrete lamp posts are the only things not constructed of wood. The large gaps between the old sleepers forming the platform appear to be sufficiently far apart to trap ladies' heels.

*c.* 1960 Lens of Sutton

# Bromyard Junction to Suckley

On 1 August 1861 an Act was passed for raising £200,000 to build a branch between Bransford Road, on the West Midland Railway's Worcester to Great Malvern line, and the Shrewsbury and Hereford Railway at Leominster. The WMR provided a quarter of the capital, but there was a certain amount of mismanagement, for on 31 March 1864 the company chairman, Sir Charles Hastings, and incidentally the founder of the British Medical Association, told the half yearly meeting that although £21,873 had been spent, not all the required land had been purchased, nor the building contract signed. On 7 October 1864 the shareholders were informed that the contract for building the Bransford to Bromyard section had been let to Yeoman of Darlaston and that work was progressing slowly. The company's engineers Wilson and Lewis reported in September 1865 that the works were 'in hand', but then on 22 December 1866 labour ceased, the contractor having been declared bankrupt. In January 1867 the contract was let to Jackson for completion. On 30 June 1867 the company's bank balance stood at only £67 and local inhabitants were invited to invest in the company in order that the line could be completed as far as Bromyard. The GWR stepped in with a loan of £40,000. In 1869 plans for carrying the line beyond Bromyard were abandoned and it was decided to make Yearsett, near Suckley, and just over the border into Herefordshire, a temporary terminus.

Almost thirteen years after the Act was passed, the Board of Trade inspected the line on 29 April 1874 and granted a certificate. Bransford Road Junction (later named Leominster Junction) to Yearsett opened on Saturday 2 May 1874, intermediate stations being at Leigh Court and Knightwick. Suckley was not ready until 1 March 1878.

As powers had lapsed, an extension from Yearsett to Bromyard was authorized by an Act of 26 May 1873 and opened on 22 October 1877, Yearsett station being closed that day and the line diverted. The life of Yearsett station was one of the briefest on record. The Worcester, Bromyard and Leominster Railway Company was dissolved and sold to the GWR on 1 July 1888, ten shillings cash being offered for each £10 ordinary share. A new company eventually extended the line from Bromyard to Leominster, which opened on 1 September 1897, thirty-six years after it was first authorized. All stations on the branch closed to passengers and goods on 7 September 1964.

The branch curved westwards from the Worcester to Hereford line at Bromyard Junction signal-box. This was renamed Leominster Junction in the 1890s and Bransford Road Junction on 25 September 1950. At this box Up trains for Worcester Tunnel Junction sounded one long and one short whistle. The branch was double for the first 286 yards in order to allow a Down train to pass an Up branch train held at the junction signals. The gradient rose at 1 in 162 from the junction to Leigh Court, a single-platformed, small, single-storey, brick-built station on the Down side. Its signal-box closed on 21 October 1956, when access to the single siding was governed by a ground frame. Over a mile

Two ex-GWR diesel railcars, W33W and W38W, joined by corridor connection and painted in BR green livery, stand at Worcester (Foregate Street) with a train from Bromyard. As the station is on a viaduct the signal-box necessarily had to be in this raised position.

4.11.61 E. Wilmshurst

beyond the station, the branch crossed Hayley Dingle Viaduct, 107 yards in length and, nearly a mile beyond that, Broad Dingle Viaduct, 93 yards long. The gradient steepened to 1 in 100 up on the approach to Knightwick. This station with a building in similar style to that at Leigh Court, also had a similar track layout, but by the 1920s an additional siding had been laid on the far side of the yard. Although Knightwick itself had a small population, the station was convenient for several hamlets and villages.

Suckley station had a timber-built office on its original single platform on the Up side, and one siding. In April 1908 a crossing loop and Down platform with a standard Great Western red-brick waiting hut were brought into use. On 21 October 1956 the signal-box was closed and three new ground frames installed. The Down line was made a goods loop and the former Up line used for trains in both directions. The Up line was chosen because it gave a straight run.

Yearsett station was just over half a mile beyond and in 1953 its location could still be traced, the foundations of the buildings showing as well as the site of the buffer stops. It appeared to have been a single-line terminus with a run-round loop, end-loading dock and sidings. The former road entrance to the station yard had been replaced by a field gate with a small wicket adjoining, the short approach slope being still paved as originally constructed. The original line diverged from the later one half a mile west of Suckley station near milepost 131 and dropped away on a course partly covered by the embankment of the later line.

In early days 517 class 0–4–2Ts worked passenger trains and 0–6–0STs headed goods. Latterly passenger trains were either worked by a 2–6–2T or 0–6–0PT and two-coach set, or, from August 1934 an 0–4–2T and auto car. The 3571 class 0–4–2T No. 3574 appeared until it was withdrawn in 1949. A GWR diesel railcar was rostered on some workings. The 2251 class 0–6–0s tended to work goods trains. Because of the gradients, all Down freight and ballast trains, except those ballast trains completely fitted with vacuum brakes, were required to be worked wherever possible with a 20 ton brake van.

At the opening of the line to Yearsett in 1874 the four trains each way daily took 35 minutes from Worcester, a distance of 10¾ miles. One train each way was 'mixed'. A similar service was run when the line was extended to Bromyard. With the opening through to Leominster in 1897, five passenger and two goods trains ran each weekday, while a Sunday service from Worcester to Bromyard was introduced in 1923, running from May to October. In 1953 six trains ran from Worcester to Bromyard (the Leominster to Bromyard section having closed 15 September 1952), plus one goods train. When the remainder of the branch closed on 7 September 1964 there were only two trains from Worcester (Shrub Hill) to Bromyard, the first of the day leaving as late as 16.10, except on Saturdays when there were two extras, the first leaving at 10.20. Three trains ran in the opposite direction Mondays to Fridays and six on Saturdays. During the season hop-pickers specials were run, usually from Birmingham or the Black Country, the stock being 'third class coaches of the oldest type'.

Gloucester Railway Carriage and Wagon Works Company motor brake second single-car DMU No. W55018 leaves Leigh Court with the 5.17 p.m. Bromyard to Worcester on the last day of passenger working. Notice the neat arrangement of the exhaust pipes.

5.9.64 Michael Mensing

No. 7004 *Eastnor Castle* works the 11.15 a.m. Paddington to Hereford express past Bransford Junction, where the branch from Bromyard is visible on the left.

8.6.63 Michael Mensing

Ex-GWR twin diesel railcars W33W and W38W at Leigh Court with a Bromyard to Worcester train. The signal-box closed on 21.10.56.

4.11.61 E. Wilmshurst

Knightwick, view Down.

*c.* 1960 Lens of Sutton

57XX class 0–6–0PT No. 8793 on Broad Dingle Viaduct east of Knightwick, working the 1850 Bromyard to Worcester (Shrub Hill). The train comprises three corridor coaches. The shed plate is 65A (Eastfield, Glasgow). Is this an error for 85A Worcester?

16.5.64 Michael Mensing

The luggage compartment doors of the twin ex-GWR diesel W33W and W38W are open at Knightwick.

4.11.61 E. Wilmshurst

57XX class 0–6–0PT No. 4664 and a B-set leave Knightwick with the morning train for Worcester. Notice the goods siding on the left and the loading gauge.

21.7.56 G. Bannister

Gloucester Railway Carriage and Wagon Company motor brake second single-car DMU No. W55003 leaves Knightwick with the 1.05 p.m. Worcester (Shrub Hill) to Bromyard.

21.3.64 Michael Mensing

Ex-GWR twin diesel units W33W and W38W at Suckley with a train for Worcester.

4.11.61 E. Wilmshurst

Ex-GWR diesel railcar No W20W leaves Suckley as the 5.23 p.m. Bromyard to Worcester (Shrub Hill). The difference between the driving bogie, right and the non-driving bogie, left, can be seen. This car, withdrawn by BR in October 1962, has been preserved on the Kent and East Sussex Railway.

9.9.61 Michael Mensing

A three-car Swindon Cross-Country DMU arriving at Suckley with the 6.50 p.m. Bromyard to Worcester (Shrub Hill).

9.9.61 Michael Mensing

A three-car Suburban DMU leaving Suckley with the 9.38 a.m. Worcester (Shrub Hill) to Bromyard.

5.10.63 Michael Mensing

# Branches at Worcester

Worcester had a fascinating 900 yard-long, steeply-graded branch. The Lowesmoor Tramway, better known as the Vinegar Branch, was built under the Worcester Railways Act of 1870 and obtained by Hill Evans and Company, vinegar manufacturers. The line opened in May or June 1872 and carried some 5000 tons annually.

From Tunnel Junction the branch passed between the two engine sheds, then crossed the main line on the level between Shrub Hill Junction and Rainbow Hill Junction. Before the Shrub Hill Road level crossing were Messrs Heenan and Froude's private sidings. In addition to securely applying wagon brakes, sprags were required to be inserted in the wheels of any wagon left in the sidings, or if more than one wagon, sprags were to jam the wheels of vehicles at the lower end. To guard against runaways when shunting at these sidings, a brake van was required at the lower end of the vehicles on the branch line as breakaways over busy level crossings could have had particularly serious consequences.

The Sectional Appendix to the Working Time Table and Books of Rules and Regulations for the Gloucester Traffic District published in October 1960 gave the procedure to be followed at Shrub Hill Road level crossing:

(a) The Driver, after bringing the train to a stand at the fixed signal protecting Shrub Hill Road Level Crossing, must sound the engine whistle, which will be an intimation to the Crossing Keeper that the train is ready to proceed to Messrs. Hill Evans' works.

(b) The Shrub Hill Road Crossing Keeper must then operate the road signals in accordance with the following instructions:–

Insert Key "X" in lock marked "X" on signal post on Shrub Hill side of road crossing, operate this key and place signal arm to Danger; hold the arm in this position by the metal handle, turn Key "Y" and withdraw it from the quadrant; take Key "Y" to the signal post on the Lowesmoor side of the road crossing, insert it in Lock "Y", operate the key, and place signal arm to Danger; hold the arm in this position by the metal handle, turn Key "Z" and withdraw it from the quadrant, Key "Z" is then available for releasing the Ground Frame locks on each side of the crossing.

(c) After the Ground Frame lock has been released and the appropriate signal lowered, the Shrub Hill Road Crossing Keeper must equip himself with flags, take up a suitable position in the public road, on the Shrub Hill Station side, and stop the movement of all traffic (including pedestrians), over the crossing by exhibiting a red flag until the train has passed complete. The Crossing Keeper is responsible for exhibiting a green hand signal by flag to the Driver as an indication that road traffic has been stopped and the train may pass over the public road.

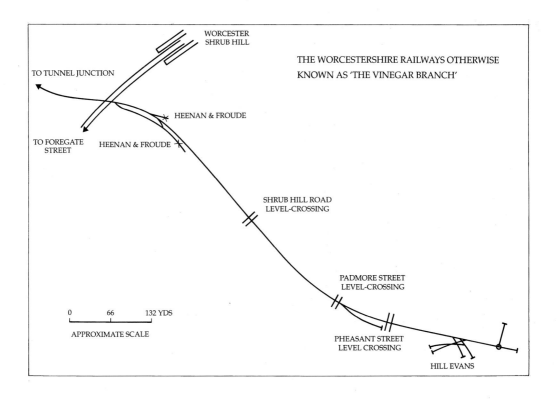

The signals referred to were standard GWR lower quadrant types and these controlled road traffic at the ungated Shrub Hill Road level crossing and Padmore Street level crossing, the latter being in close proximity to the Midland Red bus garage. They were hand-operated and left clear until a train was about to cross. During the hours of darkness, fog or falling snow, the Shrub Hill Road crossing keeper was required to place on each side of the rails one lighted hurricane lamp with a red glass. He held a hand lamp, stood on the Shrub Hill station side of the crossing and stopped all traffic. The under-shunter assisted him.

The Sectional Appendix continued:

After the Shrub Hill Road Crossing Keeper has carried out his duties connected with the safe passage of a train over Shrub Hill Road, he must proceed to Padmore Street Road Crossing and ring the electric bell fixed on a post on the Shrub Hill side of the Padmore Street Crossing, as an indication to Messrs. Hill Evans & Company that the train is ready to enter the works.

(a) The hand points situated adjacent to Padmore Street Crossing are normally set and padlocked for entrance to the Vulcan Siding.

(b) The following method of working must be carried out:

Trains proceeding to Messrs. Hill Evans' works must be brought to a stand clear of the points on the Shrub Hill side of the Vulcan Siding. The engine must then be uncoupled by the Shunter and enter the Vulcan Siding, coming to a stand on Messrs. Hill Evans' side of Padmore Street Level Crossing; the points must then be reversed by the Shunter and the wagons gravitated into Messrs. Hill Evans' Works. (Whenever possible, the gravitation movement should be brought to a stand clear of Padmore

Street Crossing so that the engine can be coupled up in the rear before the train fouls Pheasant Street Crossing.)

During the time the engine is standing in the siding to permit of vehicles being gravitated towards the Vinegar Works, the Fireman must station himself near the hand point level and see that it is not moved until the whole of the vehicles have passed safely over the points.

Note – During gravitation, a brake van in which the Guard or Head Shunter must ride must be the leading vehicle owing to lack of clearance for staff to apply brakes to moving vehicles, and to ensure absolute control of wagons entering the firm's works.

(c) After the wagons have been gravitated clear of the Vulcan Siding connection, the engine must leave the Vulcan Siding and stand clear of the points until the Crossing Keeper has again set them in the required position. The Crossing Keeper must then take up his position on the public road, see all is clear, and hand signal the Driver to proceed.

(d) No movement of engine or wagons over Padmore Street Crossing must be made until an "All Right" hand signal or lamp has been received from the Crossing Keeper in charge of crossing.

Note – The Vulcan Siding hand points must be unlocked by the Shrub Hill Road Crossing Keeper after the train has come to a stand; this man is also responsible for setting the hand points for the siding and locking them in that position as soon as practicable after the train has returned from the works and passed to Worcester Yard, and for the safe custody of the key of the padlock.

(e) The Shrub Hill Road Crossing Keeper is responsible for the protection of Padmore Street Level Crossing for the passage of Down trains during clear weather, or when fog or falling snow prevails, in precisely the same manner as for the protection of Shrub Hill Road Crossing; before signalling any movement which necessitates an engine or vehicles passing over Pheasant Street Crossing, he must satisfy himself that the appropriate fixed signal at Pheasant Street Crossing has been lowered for the movement of wagons or engine across the public highway to enter the premises of Hill Evans & Company.

Messrs. Hill Evans provide a man at Pheasant Street Public Road Level Crossing to control traffic and he will be equipped with the necessary flags and hurricane lamps with red glasses for stopping road traffic. The fixed signals situated on the Worcester (Shrub Hill) side of the crossing are operated by this man. No movement of engine or wagons on to or over the public highway must take place without the engine whistle being sounded and the Driver receiving a green hand signal by flag or lamp from the man protecting the crossing indicating the engine may pass on to or over the public road; in addition the Driver must satisfy himself the appropriate fixed signal has been lowered.

Messrs Hill Evans made shunts in their sidings with a tractor. When a train was ready to leave the vinegar works, the engine driver sounded two whistles to intimate to the Shrub Hill Road crossing keeper that it was ready to leave for Worcester Yard. On the return journey both brake vans were to be at the rear to guard against any breakaways. On both Down and Up journeys a man, that is the guard and under-shunter, was to ride in each van, except during fog or falling snow, when the latter was required to assist the Shrub Hill Road Crossing Keeper. In any weather care was to be exercised to ensure that the crossing keeper was in position to avoid a train being stopped on the steep incline between the works and Padmore Street except in a case of emergency. Up trains were required to be brought to a stand before Shrub Hill Road level crossing and procedure there was as for trains in the opposite direction.

Regarding Hill Evans' employees, the Appendix instructed that on receipt of a gong intimation from the Shrub Hill Road crossing keeper, the Hill Evans' man should open the gates of Padmore Street level crossing and return to Pheasant Street to control traffic over the public highway while the train was passing. The road signal was required to be placed at danger, and when the traffic had been brought to a stand he was to lower the railway signal.

Signals on the branch could not be treated as normal railway signals because an engine driver was not to move forward from a signal protecting a crossing after it had been lowered until he received an 'All Right' green hand signal from the crossing keeper indicating that the public highway was clear for the passage of the train. The maximum load for the branch was twelve vehicles, subject to the gross weight of the twelve vehicles not exceeding 104 tons exclusive of the two brake vans. The Appendix stated that it was very important that trips to and from the Worcester Railways worked to schedule and unless special instructions were issued, shunters were not waiting at the various works for traffic which was not ready. A return trip took about 45 minutes. The branch was often worked by 850 class 0–6–0PT No. 2007 and more recently by 16XX class engines of the same wheel arrangement. The line was last used on 5 June 1964.

Another Worcester line was the Butts and Riverside branch. It trailed from the Hereford to Worcester main line at Butts Branch Junction and descended the 553 yard-long Butts Branch Viaduct alongside the 935 yard Worcester Viaduct carrying the main line across both the valley and the River Severn. The branch then curved northwards alongside the river bank to Butts Terminus adjacent to the racecourse Grandstand Hotel. From Butts Terminus trains could reverse under the main-line Worcester Viaduct and then pass for almost half a mile along the North and South quays to Riverside Terminus. Originally used for rail/river exchange, the quay lines were closed about 1930. However, the line to Butts Terminus remained open and in the early 1940s was worked by LNER J25 0–6–0s No. 1989 and No. 2040, which were on loan to the GWR. Racehorse facilities were withdrawn on 25 April 1953 and the branch last used in 1955. It was officially closed on 1 February 1957.

The Worcester to Hereford main line crosses the River Severn, while on the left bank is the Riverside branch. Two low-sided wagons stand below the bridge, and a van and more open wagons are further on.

*c.* 1905 Author's collection

16XX class 0–6–0PT No. 1639 crosses the Shrub Hill to Foregate Street curve as it leaves the 'Vinegar Branch'. The controlling signal-box, Shrub Hill Junction, can be seen behind the locomotive carrying 'A' headlamps.

28.8.62 Michael Mensing

16XX class 0–6–0PT No. 1661 crosses Shrub Hill Road, Worcester, with a train of vans containing vinegar from Messrs Hill Evans' works. The spark-arresting cowl was fitted in 1955 when the engine was new, to enable it to work to the naval armament depot at Ditton Priors. The railway-type signal halts road traffic, the shunter holding a flag as an additional precaution. It is not known if the display of 'A' headlamps was authentic for this unusual shunting movement.

21.4.61 Ellis James-Robertson

| From WORCESTER (Foregate St.) (Continued) To | Return Fare Second Class | | From WORCESTER (Shrub Hill) (Continued) To | Return Fare Second Class | |
|---|---|---|---|---|---|
| | s. | d. | | s. | d. |
| Malvern Link | 2 | 11 | Paddington (A) | 33 | 3 |
| Newport | 21 | 6 | Pershore | 3 | 3 |
| Oxford (A) | 15 | 9 | Reading (A) | 24 | 0 |
| Paddington (A) | 33 | 3 | Stourbridge Junc. | 7 | 9 |
| Pontypool Road | 18 | 6 | Stourbridge Town | 8 | 0 |
| Reading (A) | 24 | 0 | Stratford-upon-Avon | 8 | 0 |
| Stourbridge Junc. | 7 | 9 | Weston-super-Mare | 24 | 0 |
| Stourbridge Town | 8 | 0 | Wyre Halt | 3 | 6 |
| Stratford-upon-Avon | 8 | 0 | | | |
| Weston-super-Mare | 24 | 0 | | | |
| | | | **From WYRE HALT** To | | |
| | | | Evesham | 1 | 10 |
| **From WORCESTER (Shrub Hill)** To | | | Worcester | 3 | 6 |
| Birmingham | 8 | 3 | | | |
| Bristol T.M. | 18 | 0 | | | |
| Bromsgrove | 3 | 6 | | | |
| Cheltenham | 6 | 9 | **From YATTON** To | | |
| Colwall | 3 | 9 | | | |
| Droitwich Spa | 2 | 4 | | | |
| Evesham | 5 | 0 | Bath Spa | 7 | 0 |
| Fladbury | 4 | 0 | Bedminster | 4 | 0 |
| Gloucester | 8 | 3 | Bridgwater | 7 | 6 |
| Great Malvern | 3 | 3 | Bristol T.M. | 4 | 0 |
| Hartlebury | 3 | 9 | Cardiff Gen | 14 | 3 |
| Hereford | 9 | 6 | Clevedon Halt | 1 | 6 |
| Kidderminster | 5 | 9 | Nailsea & B. | 1 | 9 |
| Ledbury | 5 | 0 | Newport | 11 | 6 |
| Malvern Link | 2 | 11 | Paddington | 35 | 9 |
| Oxford (A) | 15 | 9 | Parson Street | 4 | 0 |
| | | | Taunton | 10 | 0 |
| | | | Weston-super-Mare | 3 | 0 |

Cheap Day second class return fares advertised in a publicity handbill for 27.9.65 to 29.5.66.

# Droitwich Spa to Lye

The Droitwich to Lye section of the Worcester to Birmingham line started as a main line, but was later relegated to branch status. The Oxford, Worcester and Wolverhampton Act of 4 August 1845 authorized the construction of a line from Wolvercot Junction, Oxford via Evesham, Worcester and Kidderminster to the London and North Western Railway at Bushbury. The standard gauge line between Droitwich and Stourbridge opened on 1 May 1852, when the first train headed by 'A' (at first OWWR engines were lettered instead of numbered), a 2–4–0 hauling twenty-one coaches, left Stourbridge cheered by crowds, cannons and church bells and was grandly welcomed at the other stations en route to Evesham. Stourbridge to Dudley opened to goods traffic on 16 November 1852 and to passengers on 20 December. Through trains began running between Dudley and Oxford on 4 June 1853 and from Wolverhampton on 1 July 1854.

On 14 June 1860 an Act was obtained for constructing the Stourbridge Railway from Stourbridge through Lye to the Old Hill. The following year an agreement to work the Stourbridge Railway on its completion was made with the West Midland Railway, which had been formed from the amalgamation of the OWWR and two other companies. Stourbridge Junction to Lye and Cradley was opened on 1 April 1863, just four months before the GWR took over the WHR. An unfortunate event occurred in 1870 when, following the disappearance of the Stourbridge Railway's secretary and superintendent W.T. Adcock, it was discovered that he had issued false stock to the value of £52,000. From 1 February 1870 the Stourbridge Railway was vested in the GWR.

The LNWR's route to Birmingham was 113 miles, which the fastest expresses covered in 2 hours, but the GWR's route via Oxford was 129 ¼ miles and its best train needed 2 hours 25 minutes. On 1 July 1910 the GWR opened a new route to Birmingham via Bicester, and the distance of only 110 ½ miles allowed it to compete with the LNWR by also running expresses in 2 hours. From this date most expresses were diverted to the new line, Worcester to Wolverhampton becoming more of a branch and less main line in character.

Droitwich station opened on 18 February 1852, with the Worcester to Stoke Works Junction section first used only by the Midland Railway when some of its Gloucester to Birmingham expresses were diverted to serve Worcester, regaining their own metals at Stoke Works Junction. From 1 May 1852 OWWR trains used the Worcester to Droitwich section when the Droitwich to Stourbridge line opened on that date and Droitwich developed exchange of goods traffic with the MR. When Droitwich station was rebuilt in 1899, easy approaches were made to assist the disabled visiting the natural brine baths. The statues, urns and rustic work on the platforms were probably unique on the GWR. On 1 October 1923 the station was renamed Droitwich Spa. The Down platform was shortened in September 1966 and in July 1975 both platforms were shortened. Today there is a new red-brick office building on the Up platform. The goods shed was extended in 1905 but closed on 2 January 1967. The Stoke Works and Stourbridge lines divide just north of the station and beyond the junction are Berry Hill Sidings.

Cutnall Green Halt opened in June 1928. The platforms measuring 100 feet by 8 feet were economically made with dirt piled behind a sleeper wall, the waiting sheds being of corrugated iron. Adjacent was an Up mileage siding with a coal wharf and weighbridge, and in addition a refuge siding was provided for each of the main lines. The station closed to goods on 3 February 1964, and to passengers on 5 April 1965. At Elmley Lovatt an Up loop was opened on 6 November 1937, into which trailed Air Ministry sidings. The cost of £9480 was paid by the Ministry.

Hartlebury station was the junction with the Severn Valley line, the physical junction being situated about quarter of a mile north of the passenger station. The brick station building is situated on the Down side while the opposite platform had a brick-built waiting hut with an unusually large window. It was sensibly placed near the bottom of the foot-bridge so that passengers did not have to walk far. This foot-bridge at the Kidderminster end of the platform had steps to and from the roadway, as well as from the platforms, and so could be used by pedestrians when the level crossing gates were closed across the road. In 1910 the station was equipped with gas lighting at a cost of £300. A locomotive turntable on the north side of the level crossing was removed by 1922. In 1923 the goods yard had a second-hand weighbridge from Abersychan, north of Pontypool, installed at a cost of £140, and a 5 ton hand crane costing £125 came from Yeovil (Pen Mill). In 1924 two cattle pens were erected for £395. The same year, increased traffic in fruit demanded additional sidings at a cost of £4350 and in 1942 a new goods office was built for £1018.

Each day three to four coal trains were worked to Hartlebury by LMR locomotives, left in the sidings and 'tripped' to Stourport Power Station by a WR engine. The station closed to goods on 1 February 1965, and from 5 January 1970 lost its Severn Valley passenger traffic when these services were withdrawn. The locking frame in the station signal-box was taken out of commission on 7 November 1982 and a replacement miniature panel substituted from 28 November 1982 to control the crossing's lifting barrier.

Approaching Kidderminster the line crosses the 371 yard-long Hoobrook Viaduct. Originally built of timber, it was replaced in the 1880s with blue brick arches built alongside the original piers. At its far end were Up and Down running loops which came into use on 16 December 1937. Kidderminster Junction signal-box, situated at the junction of the line to the engine shed and Bewdley, was demolished by a derailment in June 1953 and a temporary box was in use until 25 October 1953, when a permanent replacement was opened. Kidderminster was an important rail centre with nests of goods sidings, both BR and private, wagon repair sidings and carriage sidings. The station signal-box, renewed only on 16 December 1967, closed on 15 July 1973.

As Kidderminster was such an important traffic centre, the LMS siphoned off some of this by collecting carpets from the factory, then transferring them to an LMS barge for a canal journey to Wolverhampton, where they were transhipped to rail for the last leg of the journey to station or port.

The station building at Kidderminster was a very picturesque half-timbered structure, but dry rot caused it to be demolished and replaced by a single-storey red brick and glass box. Its only saving grace is the cobbled approach road shared with the splendid SVR station. The first Kidderminster station caught fire and it is believed that the half-timbered building was really destined for Stratford-upon-Avon, but the fire caused the set of prefabricated parts to be sent to Kidderminster instead.

The first engine shed at Kidderminster was of timber construction, had a single road and opened in September 1852. Situated south-east of the passenger platform, by 1926 it was inadequate for its allocation of eighteen locomotives. Thus in 1932 it was replaced by a new shed, funds for which were provided under the Loans and Guarantees Act of 1929 in order to help relieve unemployment. Preparation of the new site involved the removal of 10,000 tons of sand which was sent to the GWR works at Swindon, Wolverhampton and Caerphilly. The new 200 ft-long double-road shed situated south of the branch to Bewdley consisted of a steel frame clad with corrugated iron sheeting. However, it was not new, but came from Bassaleg where it had been the principal depot of the Brecon and Merthyr Railway. Built in 1921, the GWR closed it on 31 March 1929 as an economy measure subsequent to the 1923 Amalgamation. The shed had the GWR code KDR, while in BR times it was 85D from 1949 to 1960, 84G from 1960 to 1963 and 2P from 1963 to 1964.

The shed generally had a stud of one or two tender engines, but most were of the tank variety, some for goods and some for passenger working. In the late 1920s one of the latter was No. 27, an ex-Midland and South Western Junction Railway 4–4–4T. In May 1947 ex-Alexandra Docks Railway 2–6–2T No. 1206 was loaned to Kidderminster to work trains to the local sugar beet factory. On 31 December 1947 sixteen locomotives were allocated, and fifteen in March 1959. The shed closed on 10 August 1964, when its remaining engines were transferred to Stourbridge Junction.

Just before Churchill and Blakedown, now simply Blakedown, the line crosses the 173 yard Blakedown Viaduct, originally timber, but replaced in engineer's blue brick in the 1880s. Today on the Up platform is a GWR nameboard surrounded by attractive-looking shrubs. The signal-box remains to control the lifting barriers. The original station building at Churchill and Blakedown was timber, later replaced by a standard GWR red brick building on the Up platform. Today it has just simple modern shelters. Hagley too, originally timber, was replaced by a GWR red-brick building on the Up platform, with a waiting room in the same style on the opposite platform. The covered foot-bridge is dated 1884. North of the station the line passes through a long cutting of Old Red Sandstone.

The original station at Stourbridge (it did not receive the Junction appellation until 1 October 1879) was situated between the junction of the branch to Stourbridge Town and the branch to Handsworth Junction. With the development of traffic, a new station was required, but this was impossible in such a cramped site. In March 1897 the GWR decided to build a new station half a mile to the south at the far end of the extensive goods yard. The original station had only two platforms, but the new junction station opened on 1 October 1901 had two island platforms, allowing four trains to use them. Today the layout has been rationalized to give platforms for Up and Down Main and for the branch line, but the station buildings are substantially unaltered, apart from heavy-looking new roofs to the platform canopies. The opening of this new station caused the branch to be re-aligned so that it curved south instead of north to join the main line. This new route was used from the date of the opening of the new station. Together with the new passenger station, goods and livestock accommodation at Stourbridge Junction was improved and a goods line laid avoiding the passenger station.

At the north end of the goods sidings the original line to Wolverhampton, now the freight line to Dudley, curves left while the Stourbridge Railway carries straight on and proceeds to Lye. There the two-road, GWR standard red-brick station had a waiting shelter on the Down platform. Today the offices are contained in a modern flat-roofed building on the Up platform quite lacking in character. At one time Lye had a large goods shed, with the yard equipped with a modern travelling crane, and there were brickworks sidings at both ends of the station. Hayes Lane Junction signal-box, situated over a quarter of a mile beyond Lye passenger station, closed in November 1887, the junction being moved nearer the station so that it could be worked from Lye signal-box. From its opening in June 1863, the three-quarters of a mile Hayes Lane branch curved southwards to serve several collieries and brickworks. Most of the branch closed in April 1962 and the remaining stub on 10 August 1964.

The line to Dudley crosses the 190 yard-long Stourbridge Viaduct, originally of timber, but replaced by a new brick structure completed on 14 April 1882. Almost immediately beyond was Engine House signal-box controlling the junction with the incline line, closed in 1879, to Stourbridge Goods. Beside this branch, and half a mile from the Junction station, was Stourbridge Junction engine shed. The original four-road straight shed with brick walls opened in 1870, and had an allocation of forty-two engines on 1 January 1901. It closed when a GWR standard depot with stabling roads leading from a central turntable was opened in 1926. The new shed was erected by a local builder, A.H. Guest. The old building was retained for use by steam railmotors and trailers, and after their withdrawal was used by diesel railcars. It remained in use, even being partly renewed in 1957 to service DMUs. On 31 December 1947 eighty-four engines were allocated to the depot, but this decreased to sixty-four in March 1959 and thirty-three in May 1965. It closed on 11 July 1966, most of the locomotives being transferred to Tyseley, Oxley, Croes Newydd and Rose Grove. Stourbridge Junction shed, originally GWR code STB, became BR 84F and then 2C in 1963.

Stourbridge Junction is the terminus for some Up trains and timetables show an increasing frequency of service through the years. In August 1887 nine trains ran between Lye and Stourbridge Junction and ten in the reverse direction, trains on Sundays being five and four respectively. Twelve ran between Droitwich and Stourbridge Junction and thirteen in the Up direction throughout the week. By April 1910 there were no fewer than twenty-four trains scheduled each way between Lye and Stourbridge Junction, and seven each way on Sundays. On weekdays the number of trains between Droitwich and Stourbridge Junction remained the same, while the four each way on Sundays was worse. In July 1922 the service from Lye had increased to thirty-one trains, with twenty-nine Down, other services remaining the same. July 1938 saw even better frequencies, with thirty-eight Up trains from Lye, thirty-five Down and fourteen each way on Sundays. Between Droitwich and Stourbridge Junction there were twenty-two trains, with twenty in the opposite direction and ten each way on Sundays. The timetable for winter 1994 shows thirty Up trains Lye to Stourbridge and twenty-six Down, and none on Sundays as the station is closed. Thirty-three ran each way between Stourbridge Junction and Droitwich and ten on Sundays.

The BR passenger service south of Kidderminster had loadings so light that closure between Stourbridge Junction and Worcester was seriously contemplated, but when HSTs were introduced on Bristol–Gloucester–Birmingham services from 16 May 1983, local trains from Gloucester to Birmingham, which hitherto had travelled via Bromsgrove, were re-routed via Kidderminster in order to leave a clearer path. The new stopping service had semi-fasts from Birmingham to Worcester stopping only at Cradley Heath, Stourbridge Junction, Kidderminster and Droitwich, and hourly stopping trains between Birmingham and Kidderminster.

The line suffered an unusually high number of accidents and mishaps during its early years, the first occurring on the opening day, 1 May 1852. About 7.00 p.m. half of the directors enjoying the celebratory dinner at the Lion Hotel, Kidderminster, decided to go to Droitwich to catch an MR connection. As the engine driver could not be found – no doubt he was having his own celebration – David Joy, the OWWR's locomotive engineer, drove 2–4–0 engine 'A' to Droitwich and dropped off his passengers. While running round the train before returning to Kidderminster, at the Down end of the station the engine dropped tender-first off the bridge over the Droitwich Canal. It was not Joy's fault, but the station-master's who had turned the wrong set of points. The contractor's engine *Jack of Newbury* hauled Joy back onto the road.

Two accidents occurred on the timber Hoobrook Viaduct, Kidderminster. A coupling rod fractured, the two ends punching holes through the viaduct's 3 inch-thick deck planking. A similar fracture happened to a connecting rod while OWWR 0–4–2 *Canary* was crossing tender-first. A broken end crashed through the firebox, causing scalding water and steam to flood back on the train.

OWWR 2–4–0 No. 25 was heading a heavy coal train from Dudley and ran away down the bank into Droitwich. Joe Leedham was its driver, usually referred to as 'Hell Fire Dick' because of his love for speed. As he approached the junction signal it turned from white (clear) to red, giving him no chance to stop, especially as he had only four instead of six coupled wheels. Simultaneously he observed a mail train approaching on the converging line. He had only one chance to avoid a collision. Hell Fire Dick threw open his regulator and the mineral train rushed through the junction ahead of the mail, thus averting a collision.

One advantage of rails being laid on longitudinal, as opposed to cross, sleepers was that in the event of a derailment, derailed trains tended to remain upright. One OWWR passenger engine travelling at about 40 mph near Stourbridge Junction broke its front axle, but due to the track being on longitudinal sleepers, remained upright.

Another incident near Stourbridge Unction occurred in pre-block signalling days while David Joy was riding on the footplate of 2–4–0 No. 26 travelling 'light'. As they speeded round a curve they were shocked to see before them a gang of permanent way men on a trolley. Driver George Emby reversed the engine, and the firemen screwed down the tender brakes till, as Joy described it in his diary, 'the water, thrown forward, poured out of the tender like a river. The navvies in no time tipped up the trolley from the "6-foot" and toppled it, going with it down into the ditch, and we rolled over the spot a second later – all right'.

The OWWR was not unfairly known as the 'Old Worse & Worse', for on 18 October 1855, the 6.45 p.m. express from Oxford to Wolverhampton needed four engines before it could leave Hartlebury. The train engine, 2–4–0 No. 14, was stopped by a tyre jamming against the firebox. The station-master telegraphed to Kidderminster and within half an hour its replacement arrived, 2–4–0 No. 25. Unfortunately the driver could not close his regulator and so proceeded on to Worcester where he reported the problem. The next engine to try and move the train was 0–6–0 No. 10, nicknamed 'Mother Shuter'. This was the Worcester (Shrub Hill) pilot and was driven by no less than David Joy himself. She was coupled up and about to proceed when her water gauge glass blew out, and when Joy attempted to shut off steam from the gauge, one of the studs blew out and yet another engine had to be sent from Worcester. The train eventually arrived at Wolverhampton six hours late.

Another entry in Joy's diary recounts an incident when he had his sleep disturbed.

2–4–0 No 14, with George Benson taking the 9.35 pm down to Dudley, broke a trailing tyre out beyond Hartlebury. I had got to bed when the shedman tickled my window with the usual long stick with the little bunch of wire at the end. Shedman: 'Engine off at Hartlebury'. I: 'Get No 20 ready'. I, to my housekeeper: 'Richardson, coffee and toast smart.' Then I dressed and found the meal ready. Gulped it quickly and slipped down to the shed, just below me, to find No 20 crawling out of the shed with 20 lb of steam only. Joe Lester, my man was there, also Adcock, general manager, shivering in the cold, and others. Joe said he could 'pick her up', so we started with 20 lb steam, and this time a 'hook on the block'. Before we were 10 miles away, past Droitwich, we were springing away like a bird. Arrived at the accident and found it an awfully narrow shave. The trailing tyre had broken through, but held in the one open ring hanging on the engine, till she stuck in the longitudinal timbers, stopping quietly, almost without shaking the passengers. The traffic department took them and handled them, and we tackled the engine and tender to get them out of the way; it was 12 midnight.'

Droitwich Spa, view Up.

*c.* 1960 Lens of Sutton

No. 4904 *Binnegar Hall* passes Droitwich Spa goods shed with a Sunday excursion to Cardiff. Notice the barrow crossing in the foreground formed from old sleepers, and the signal-box behind the last coach adjacent to the junction of the Stoke Works Junction line.

9.9.56 Michael Mensing

Cutnall Green, view towards Droitwich Spa. The platform wall was built of old sleepers, then soil was tipped behind and topped with gravel. The Down refuge siding can be seen on the right.

*c*. 1960 Lens of Sutton

Hartlebury, view from the level crossing. A goods train is on the Up line. Notice that the foot-bridge can be used by public and passengers alike. The waiting shelter on the left has an unusually large window. Notice the GWR monogram in both sides of the foot-bridge.

*c*. 1930 Lens of Sutton

Hartlebury, view Down. The level crossing is immediately beyond the foot-bridge and a horsebox is in the siding on the far right. There is a wheel at the top of the signal post for lowering the lamp. The distant signal arm is painted red. The signal-box has an 'S' plate showing, a black letter on a white ground to indicate to a linesman the state of the signalling apparatus.

*c.* 1905 Paul Strong collection

A similar view taken about ninety years later from the opposite platform. The signal-box still stands, but the crossing gates have been replaced by lifting barriers, the lower quadrant signal by colour light, the foot-bridge has been removed, and the station building is no longer used for railway purposes, passengers using a bus-stop-type shelter.

5.2.94 Author

The buildings on the Down platform, Hartlebury, now used by Shakespeare International Marine Limited.

5.2.94 Author

0–6–2Ts lined up outside Kidderminster locomotive shed: No. 6667, No. 5651 and an unidentified 56XX class 0–6–2T.

30.9.56 Hugh Ballantyne

Hoobrook Viaduct, Kidderminster: the original timber viaduct in the background is being replaced by a brick structure.

*c.* 1882 Author's collection

The attractive exterior of the station at Kidderminster.

*c.* 1900 Author's collection

No. 6814 *Enborne Grange* passes through Kidderminster with an Up fitted freight.

30.8.62 Michael Mensing

The exterior of the replacement building at Kidderminster.

5.2.94 Author

Kidderminster, view Down. The platform has been extended beyond the overbridge. Notice the glass in the platform canopy gives an airy appearance to the area below. The photograph appears to have been intended as a Christmas card.

*c.* 1905 Lens of Sutton

Derby Works three-car Suburban DMU with motor second W50094 leading, arrives at Kidderminster with the Sunday 1.55 p.m. Birmingham (Snow Hill) to Stourport-on-Severn.

30.3.58 Michael Mensing

Passengers at Kidderminster await a Down train. An upper quadrant signal can be seen this side of the very large former goods shed, now the SVR carriage works.

5.2.94 Author

Three-car Sprinter 150 017 stops at Kidderminster with the 1228 Hereford to Birmingham (New Street).

5.2.94 Author

The fact that the LMS did not have a line to Kidderminster did not prevent it seeking traffic – it had a goods receiving office. See photograph at the top of p. 96.

c. 1930 LMS

Here export carpets are being loaded onto an LMS barge at Kidderminster for a canal journey to Wolverhampton where they will be transferred to rail. They have been brought by an LMS mechanical horse and trailer, which can just be seen on the right. The LMS boatage depot is in the background.

*c.* 1935 Author's collection

The 173 yard-long Blakedown Viaduct a few years before it was replaced in brick.

1877 Author's collection

The attractive approach to the Up platform of Hagley station.

*c.* 1910 Author's collection

The station and approach has changed little during the last eighty-five years.

5.2.94 Author

Hagley, view Down. Note the extreme height of the home signal and its offside location to ensure visibility above two bridges.

*c.* 1910 Author's collection

Hagley, view Down. The station has changed very little over the years – mainly the removal of the supplementary timber buildings, and the signal-box, which closed on 21 April 1968.

5.2.94 Author

Hagley. The centre decoration on the foot-bridge below the top flight of steps is the date of its building, 1884. '117' is the bridge number.

5.2.94 Author

Sprinter 150 011 at Hagley with the 1158 Great Malvern to Birmingham (New Street). The passengers have just boarded.

5.2.94 Author

Staff at the original station at Stourbridge Junction.

*c*. 1900 Lens of Sutton

An 0 6 0 at Stourbridge Junction with an Up passenger train. The original card was postmarked 11.11.04.

*c*. 1902 Paul Strong collection

Stourbridge Junction: on the left Sprinter 150 102 with the 1227 Stourbridge Junction to Birmingham (New Street), and on the right, Sprinter 150 120 with the 1211 Birmingham (New Street) to Stourbridge Junction.

5.2.94 Author

The timber Stourbridge Viaduct. The brick piers of its replacement are being erected in the foreground.

1881 Author's collection

Stourbridge Junction shed, left to right: 14XX class 0–4–2T No. 1458, 57XX class 0–6–0PTs Nos 5719 and 9636, 43XX class 2–6–0 No. 4326, all at their home shed, 84F.

30.9.56 Hugh Ballantyne

'Badminton' class 4 4 0 No. 4109 *Monarch* near Stourbridge with a stopping train. Notice the vacuum reservoir on the roof of the first vehicle, which is a slip coach.

January 1925 Author's collection

Board announcing facilities offered at Stourbridge Junction.

5.2.94 Author

2021 class 0–6–0ST No. 2109 at Stourbridge Junction. Notice the tarpaulin rolled up on the cab roof. In inclement weather it could be rolled out and fixed to the upright at the rear of the bunker. These engines were known as 'Get wets'. The distant signal was painted red.

*c.* 1925 Author's collection

Lye: steam railmotor No. 5 works an Up train. Its sides are of vertical matchboarding.

*c.* 1906 Author's collection

A three-car Suburban DMU arrives at Lye with the 1503 Kidderminster to Lichfield (City).

2.4.77 Michael Mensing

Two three-car Suburban DMUs working the 1114 Lichfield (City) to Kidderminster arrive at Lye.

3.9.77 Michael Mensing

Sprinter 150 017 passes the former goods shed as it approaches Kidderminster with the 1228 Hereford to Birmingham (New Street).

5.2.94 Author

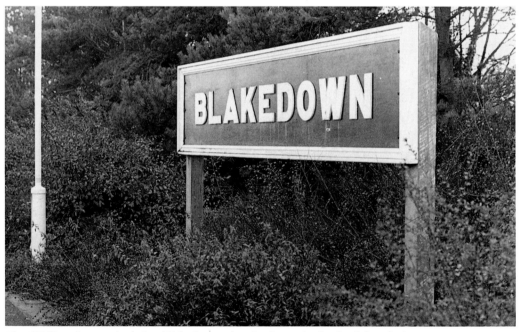

The GWR-style nameboard at Blakedown. the shrubs at the back of the platform are an attractive touch.

5.2.94 Author

A three-car Suburban DMU working the 1635 Worcester (Foregate Street) to Birmingham (New Street) leaves Stourbridge Junction and curves towards Lye.

17.1.78 Michael Mensing

Sprinter 150014 passes Lye with the 1130 Birmingham (New Street) to Hereford. the roof of the former goods shed can be seen above the DMU.

5.2.94 Author

Sprinter 150 008 passes Hartlebury with the 1428 Great Malvern to Birmingham (New Street).

5.2.94 Author

Sprinter 150011 arrives at Hagley with the 1158 Great Malvern to Birmingham (New Street). Most passengers greet it with indifference.

5.2.94 Author

# Hartlebury to Arley – The Severn Valley Railway

The original plan for the Severn Valley Railway was to leave Hartlebury, 11 miles north of Worcester, and run beside the River Severn to Shrewsbury. An Act of 20 August 1853 authorized a capital of £600,000, with borrowing powers of £200,000. Robert Nicholson was appointed engineer, and a contractor, Samuel Morton Peto, the company's chairman in May 1854. Peto held £225,000 worth of shares and at the time was constructing at cost price a military railway in the Crimea, and this act gained him a baronetcy in December 1854. On 9 May 1855 Nicholson died aged forty-six and was replaced by John Fowler, later Metropolitan Railway engineer and joint engineer to the Forth Bridge. In 1855, despite the fact that the Mayor of Bridgnorth had rather optimistically stated that 'no more remunerative line would be found in the kingdom', there were relatively few subscribers and economies were planned by making deviations and only laying a single line. A new SVR Act received Royal Assent on 30 July 1855, allowing a capital of £480,000 and borrowing powers of £160,000. Abandonment of the scheme was seriously considered in 1856, but then the OWWR offered to assist and the contractors Brassey, Peto and Betts agreed to construct the line on reasonable terms and accept part payment in shares.

They started work in 1858 and one of the first works was the viaduct over the River Stour between Hartlebury and Stourport. Although only single track was laid initially, overbridges, masonry underbridges and viaducts were built for double track, though tunnels and the rest of the line were on a single-track formation.

Two miles from Hartlebury the line cut through a sandstone ridge. This required a cutting about a third of a mile in length with a maximum depth of 60 feet. It was made in an unusual manner. A tunnel was cut, then a wagon placed under an intermediate shaft down which spoil was shovelled until the wagon was full, when it was replaced by an empty one. This cunning method avoided men having to lift spoil into the trucks, gravity doing most of the work. A cutting, rather than a tunnel, was necessary to yield sufficient spoil to form an embankment in the Stour valley.

The foundation stone of the Victoria Bridge across the River Severn near Arley, was laid appropriately by Henry Orlando Bridgeman, resident engineer, on 24 November 1859. At that time its span of 200 feet was the largest cast-iron arch in the United Kingdom.

Wet weather during the winter of 1860–1 caused several landslips. Unfortunately serious accidents occurred during construction. On 23 January 1860 a navvy lost an eye and a part of his nose when timber fell on him in Mount Pleasant Tunnel. On 9 January 1861 James Bishop was killed by rocks being blasted in the cutting south of the tunnel, while on 9 March 1861 a navvy working in a cutting south of the Victoria Bridge was lucky to escape death when a 20 lb clod of earth fell on him from a height of about 30 feet. Eventually the works neared completion and it is recorded that on 1 May 1861 a locomotive and twelve ballast wagons passed Bewdley for the first time. Colonel

William Yolland made the Board of Trade inspection at the end of December 1861, but failed to pass the line, his main criticism concerning the signalling. The line passed re-inspection on 15 January 1862. The SVR was formally opened on 31 January 1862, a 22-coach special leaving Worcester (Shrub Hill). Public services worked by the West Midland Railway began the following day. The SVR was absorbed by the GWR on 18 July 1872.

To improve the connection from the Birmingham area to the Tenbury branch, it was decided to lay a direct loop from Kidderminster to the southern end of Sandbourne Viaduct, Bewdley. Powers for this were given by the West Midland and Severn Valley Company's Act, 1 August 1861, which authorized the raising of £60,000 by shares and £20,000 by borrowing powers. The London and North Western Railway was to have running powers over the line. Edward Wilson, the OWWR's engineer, was appointed engineer to the new company. As both the Tenbury branch and the SVR were still under construction, work on the loop was held in abeyance.

In 1867 Michael Lane, the Great Western's Chief Civil Engineer, redrew plans for the loop as it had come under the auspices of the GWR in 1863. It was authorized in a GWR Act of 31 July 1868, but the company was not anxious to begin construction work and the tender of Charles Dickinson for £39,800 was not accepted until 7 October 1874. Eventually the line was finished and Colonel Rich, who carried out the Board of Trade inspection on 22 March 1878, was 'surprised and much amused' to find Bewdley Tunnel lit by candles and naphtha lamps. Although he praised highly the bridges and viaducts, the incompletion of other works caused him to decide not to issue a certificate. A second inspection was made on 29 May 1878 and on 1 June 1878 the line between Kidderminster and Bewdley was opened without ceremony.

Competition arrived on 23 May 1898 with the opening of the Kidderminster and Stourport Electric Tramway, one of the first in Great Britain. Much of its track was on sleepers at the roadside. The electric cars hauled trailers and had the first platform vestibules in the country. This tramway caused interference with the GWR's telecommunications and special insulation was required at a cost of £44, this being paid by the British Electric Traction Co. Ltd, the line's owners.

The line between Shrewsbury and Bewdley closed to passengers on 9 September 1963 and through goods trains were withdrawn on 30 November 1963. Although Highley Colliery north of Arley closed on 31 January 1969, the line between the colliery and Bewdley remained open for a few days for the removal of empty wagons, the last regular train running on 6 February. Before the line's closure, the wage packets of employees on the branch line were delivered by the engine working the goods train, but following closure on 6 February, a class 25 diesel-electric locomotive bearing the headcode 8T91 formerly carried by the branch goods, ran light from Kidderminster to Highley station every Thursday afternoon for the sole purpose of taking a wage packet to the signalman and another to the shunter who were still stationed at Highley and had nothing to do all the week! The local press commented: 'Two men operate the diesel and a guard carries the money. The diesel runs from Kidderminster to Highley, thirteen miles, at a cost of 6 shillings per mile for fuel alone, so even without the pay for these three men the round trip costs at least £7 10s 0d. To send the wages by post would cost three shillings and fivepence. Footnote: a third man, a lengthsman, is also stationed here and lives in a house alongside the track; the wages "special" stops outside his door, but he is not paid from it. He travels to Bewdley to collect his wages – on a platelayer's trolley!'

BR commented that it had no idea of how long the men were to be kept there, but it would have been uneconomical to remove them and finally close the line because within a few weeks the National Coal Board might have had scrap to move from the colliery.

Another purpose of the train travelling over the line was to ensure that everything was in order and no vandalism had taken place.

A passenger service continued to run between Kidderminster, Bewdley and Hartlebury until 5 January 1970. Coal traffic to Stourport power station ended in March 1979 and the line closed completely from 12 January 1981.

North of Hartlebury station the single track Severn Valley Railway curved north-westwards away from the double-track line to Kidderminster. At Leapgate Siding ground frame, 1½ miles north of the junction, the trailing Leapgate Siding served the Regent Oil Company's depot between 28 August 1939 and 4 January 1970. Up to thirty wagons led by a brake van were permitted to be pushed from Stourport. Beyond Leapgate was Sand Siding, and following the closure of the sand quarry this siding was used for storing coal wagons for Stourport power station. The 73 yard-long Weldon Viaduct and the 37 yard Timber Viaduct were crossed, and before passing over the Staffordshire and Worcestershire Canal on a 33 foot-span bridge, a double-track section began, a siding opened in 1940 from the Central Electricity Generating Board's works trailing into the Down line. The CEGB had two 0–4–0STs, one built by Barclay and the other by Peckett.

In the last century a siding to which access was gained by wagon turntable ran parallel with the Staffordshire and Worcestershire Canal on the west side of the line and was used for exchange traffic, but traffic developed to such an extent that in 1885 the GWR paid for a basin and warehouse. Two sidings served this basin situated on the east side of the branch. Iron and steel from South Wales and coal from Highley Colliery further up the SVR, were brought to this basin for transit to Wilden Iron Works. Latterly Stourport, renamed Stourport-on-Severn in October 1934, had a sizeable goods yard south of the passenger station, its coal yard being to the north. An economy was made on 1 April 1951 when Stourport South signal-box closed and the North signal-box had its frame extended. At the north end of the complex where the double track became single, one private siding led to Steatite and Porcelain Products Limited's works, and beyond a siding trailed in from the National Cold Stores.

The line rose at 1 in 150 to Burlish Halt situated on the Down side of the line. The halt, with a concrete platform, corrugated iron pagoda and electric lighting, opened on 31 March 1930 at a cost of £300 for engineering, £80 for the Chief Mechanical Engineer's expenses and £50 for the land. The siding to the porcelain works passed behind the halt.

The branch passed through a sandstone cutting and descended at 1 in 100 through the 123 yard-long and 85½ ft beneath the surface Mount Pleasant Tunnel. The cutting at its north end was made wide in order to provide sufficient spoil for making the embankment beyond. The loop from Kidderminster, now part of the preserved SVR, came in and the two lines ran parallel across Sandbourne Viaduct, 101 yards long, before the double track began. Bewdley bypass was crossed on a skew bridge of 60 ft span. The 2500 ton concrete bridge was pushed about 150 ft into position on 6 November 1986 and first used by trains on 29 November.

The Up platform at Bewdley is an island, thus giving the station three platform faces. The opening of the Kidderminster loop in 1878 required the enlargement of the island platform and provision of a foot-bridge to cope with the additional traffic. Bewdley became very busy with over sixty trains using it daily. A whistle code was used:

| | |
|---|---|
| For SVR Up and Down | 1 whistle |
| To and from the Tenbury line | 2 whistles |
| To and from Kidderminster | 3 whistles |

Bewdley closed to goods on 1 February 1965.

Northwood Halt, its platform a sleeper wall backfilled with spoil and surmounted by a timber waiting shelter, opened on 17 June 1935. It was situated on the Up side of the line. The SVR crosses the River Severn by means of the Victoria Bridge. It is a splendid structure in a scenic setting. The 200 ft span has four ribs, each rib consisting of nine segments. The total weight of iron in the bridge comes to about 500 tons. It is inscribed 'Messrs Brassey & Co, Contractors, Victoria Bridge 1861. John Fowler, Engineer. Cast and erected by the Coalbrookdale Company'. When it was painted in 1980 264 gallons were required. As the ends of the cast-iron girders and the cross-bracing had become corroded and the stone blocks bearing the girders cracked, early in 1994 £200,000 was spent on restoration. Not far beyond the bridge is Arley, a simple crossing loop with two sidings. The passenger station has a yellow-brick building with a slated roof. Arley originally had one platform on the east side, the second platform opening in June 1883, and both were lengthened in 1907. In 1938 a camping coach was parked at the station for use by holiday-makers. Despite the accident at Abermule on 26 January 1921 when two trains collided head-on on the Cambrian Railways single line due to confusion caused by the tablet instruments being kept in the station booking office instead of the signal-box, they remained in the booking office at Arley until the SVR preservationists wisely transferred them to the signal-box. Arley closed to goods on 9 September 1963. Today Arley is a most attractive station and has a large picnic area garden. Half a mile north the SVR enters Shropshire.

The whistle code at Kidderminster Junction was:

|  |  |
|---|---|
| To main line Up and Down | 1 whistle |
| To and from branch line | 2 whistles |

From Kidderminster Junction the single-track loop to Bewdley, falling at 1 in 112, curved past the locomotive depot, now a housing estate, crossed the Worcester Road by a 30 ft-span brick arch and went over the 132 yard Kidderminster Viaduct, consisting of seven red-brick arches of 46 ft span over the River Stour and the Staffordshire and Worcestershire Canal. At the far end of the viaduct the line rose at 1 in 114 to Foley Park Halt, the sleeper platform having a corrugated iron pagoda. Opened on 2 January 1905, it was originally situated on the south side of the line, but construction of sidings caused it to be moved to the other side of the track. The sidings led to the British Sugar Corporation's factory and were in use between 1929 and 1980. Loaded trains of sugar beet descended to Foley Park from Kidderminster with the brake van leading. The return up the gradient with about seventy empties and a van set the 0–6–0PT a considerable task.

Beyond was Rifle Range Halt, opened in June 1905 at a cost of £145 and closed on 4 October 1920. The line descended at 1 in 100 through the 486 yard-long Bewdley Tunnel. In 1910 it required a new arch of blue brick at a cost of £3247. The line was kept open and forty men were at work each night from 3 August until 20 October 1910, the scaffolding having to be removed before the first train in the morning. North of the tunnel the line ran parallel with the branch from Hartlebury and Stourport and crossed the 101 yard-long Sandbourne Viaduct, its ten brick arches resting on sandstone piers.

In the 1880s the SVR passenger service was important enough to be worked by tender engines and bogie clerestory stock at a period when many branches had to be content with tank engines hauling four-wheelers. Locomotives known to have worked SVR passenger trains in the last century were four double-framed WMR 2–4–0s Nos 93-96 (GWR Nos 190–193); GWR 171 class double-framed 2–4–0s; Standard Goods 0–6–0s; 927 class 0–6–0s; 439 class 2–4–0s; 2021 class 2–4–0s; and Metro class 2–4–0Ts. One interesting

The exterior of Stourport-on-Severn station.

*c.* 1900 Author's collection

engine was ex-Midland and South Western Junction Railway 4–4–4T GWR No. 27 which, following rebuilding with a GWR boiler in 1925, often worked Bewdley to Snow Hill trains. During the 1930s 2301 class 0–6–0s appeared and in the Second World War Collett 0–6–0s worked passenger services, as did GWR diesel railcars Nos 19, 25 and 33. LNER J25 class 0–6–0s Nos 2059, 2061 and 2142, on loan to the GWR, worked some goods trains. In the postwar era 51XX and 45XX 2–6–2Ts were to be seen, together with 2251 class 0–6–0s and 'Duke' class 4–4–0s No. 3273 *Mounts Bay* and No. 3276. Latterly 57XX class 0–6–0PTs and ex-LMS Class 2 2–6–2Ts provided motive power.

With the opening of the line in February 1862, three trains ran each way daily on the SVR, taking about 31 minutes between Hartlebury and Arley, a frequency increased after the experience of the first few months to four. A Sunday service of a solitary train each way was introduced in March 1862. In 1876 two weekday and one Sunday train ran through to Worcester. In 1904 six through trains were offered plus one between Bridgnorth and Hartlebury. This frequency lasted for many years. In 1947 only one through train ran from Shrewsbury to Hartlebury, with three in the reverse direction, other trains requiring passengers to change. In 1960 a service of three trains was provided between Arley and Hartlebury, with four in the other direction.

On 29 December 1904 a steam railmotor ran a trial service from Kidderminster to Bewdley and Stourport, with a regular service starting on 2 January 1905 using two motors. By 1910 there were nine Down and ten Up trains daily and one Up on Sundays, all taking about 20 minutes for the journey of 6¼ miles. As a reversal was necessary at Bewdley, railmotors were ideal for operating this service. By 1938 the auto service declined to four to Stourport and seven return.

The new Severn Valley Railway was incorporated on 24 May 1967 and has become one of the largest preserved railways in Britain, with six stations, over thirty steam engines and more than half a dozen diesels. Passengers can enjoy beautiful scenery not visible from roads. Passenger services began on 23 May 1970 between Bridgnorth and Hampton Loade, all of this track being in Shropshire. The line was extended to Highley on 12 April 1974, and to Bewdley on 18 May the same year, the first trip being made by ex-GWR railcar No. 22 and the first SVR steam train to Bewdley by 0–6–0PT No. 5764. The SVR flourished and grew to a membership of 5000 by 1974 and 9029 by the end of 1979. In 1984 the link with BR at Kidderminster opened. On the site of part of the former goods yard the SVR erected a new terminal passenger station building of red brick, relieved by grey brick around window and door openings. It was based on an 1890 design for Ross-on-Wye by J.E. Danks of the GWR Civil Engineer's Department. It has a double-faced platform. The first passenger train to visit for clearance tests arrived behind No. 6960 *Raveningham Hall* on 27 July 1984 and the station opened three days later. On 12 December 1984 the junction with BR was passed for passenger traffic and the first through working took place on 29 December. The new station building, as opposed to just the platform, opened to the public on 28 September 1985, though its official opening was not until 4 July 1986. In 1985 the former goods shed at Kidderminster was purchased for use by the SVR's Carriage and Wagon Department, and at the end of 1986 a new Kidderminster Station signal-box with a 62-lever frame was opened.

Stourport-on-Severn, view Down, with the coal yard siding on the left. The grating in the foreground is to catch any water from the bag of the water crane. Notice the centre-pivotted signals used in this confined location. The signal-box is Stourport North. The DMU has just arrived from Hartlebury.

3.2.68 D. Payne

The first steam railmotor to arrive at Stourport, probably No. 25. Notice the clean buffers and polished cylinder cover. Bystanders find the photographer more interesting than the railmotor.

29.12.04 Paul Strong collection

51XX class 2–6–2T No. 5153 at Stourport-on-Severn with a Down goods train. This photograph is taken from the foot-bridge, which was used when the level crossing gates were closed across the road. Notice that the signal-box has been extended at its far end. The water tank is mushroom-shaped.

*c.* 1960 Lens of Sutton

Burlish Halt with its corrugated iron pagoda hut; view towards Stourport. The distant signal is for Bewdley South.

*c.* 1960 Lens of Sutton

Andrew Barclay 0–4–0ST, No. 2088 *Sir Thomas Royden*, built in 1940, shunts at Stourport power station.

21.6.70 Hugh Ballantyne

Ex-LMS class 8 2–8–0 No. 8233 arrives at Kidderminster with empty stock for the 1155 departure.

13.10.88 Author

Final preparations being made for the official opening of the new Severn Valley Railway station at Kidderminster on the following day. A works train is headed by the SVR-owned 08 class shunter D3022 in BR green livery. The station was built on the site of part of the former BR goods yard. The SVR erected the station buildings subsequently.

29.7.84 Hugh Ballantyne

The splendid GWR-style new station building provided by the SVR at Kidderminster. The paved approach road gives the required period look.

5.2.94 Author

A GWR pump trolley at Kidderminster. Pumping the handles up and down enabled permanent way men to proceed to the length where they were to work. The footbrake can be seen protruding up between the two wheels. The trolley was lifted clear of the running line by the handles provided at each end.

13.10.88 Author

The corrugated iron pagoda at Foley Park: view towards Bewdley. The platform is made from old sleepers. The overbridge is wide enough for double track. One of the sugar factory sidings can be seen on the left.

*c.* 1965 Lens of Sutton

Gloucester Railway Carriage and Wagon Company single car DMU W55005, left, with the 4.20 p.m. Shrewsbury to Hartlebury, and W55004 on the right, about to leave Bewdley for Bridgnorth. The goods shed and loading dock can be seen on the right.

6.9.63 Hugh Ballantyne

Bewdley, view towards Hartlebury. The train on the left is probably for Woofferton Junction. In the centre is a steam railmotor bound for Kidderminster or Hartlebury, while on the right is a tank engine probably heading a train for Shrewsbury. The foot-bridge has shallow girders.

*c.* 1910 Author's collection

Bewdley: railmotor No. 91 in brown livery. An LNWR through coach is at the rear of a Woofferton Junction to Birmingham train. Its roof board reads, 'Through Carriage between Birmingham and Woofferton via Smethwick'.

*c.* 1909 Author's collection

Ex-GWR diesel railcar W22W arriving at Bewdley, with a three-car DMU on the viaduct. Notice the centre-pivotted signals in front of the signal-box.

15.8.59 Michael Mensing

A visitor to the SVR was LNWR 'Coal Tank' 0–6–2T No. 1054. Here it passes Bewdley South signal-box with the 1000 Bridgnorth to Kidderminster. The signalman is about to hand over the single-line tablet for Kidderminster.

19.9.86 Hugh Ballantyne

The 1645 Kidderminster to Bridgnorth arrives at Bewdley behind class 2MT 2–6–0 No. 46443.

13.10.88 Author

45XX class 2–6–2T No. 4566 arrives at Bewdley with the 1610 Bridgnorth to Kidderminster.

13.10.88 Author

Ivatt class 4MT 2–6–0 No. 43106 at Bewdley. The tender cab, which helped to ease conditions when running tender-first, can be clearly seen.

21.10.76 Revd Alan Newman

Ex-GWR 28XX class 2–8–0 No. 2857 at Bewdley.

13.10.88 Author

Ex-GWR 0–6–0ST No. 813 at Bewdley, minus its coupling rods. This engine was formerly owned by the Port Talbot Railway and Docks Company.

13.10.88 Author

The unusually wide platform at Northwood Halt, view towards Arley. The sign at the end of the platform reads, 'No Road'.

*c*. 1965 Lens of Sutton

BR Standard class 3 2–6–2T No. 82004 approaches Bewdley with the 1.45 p.m. Shrewsbury to Hartlebury. The branch to Suckley and Woofferton Junction falls away to the left.

20.6.59 Michael Mensing

Class 2MT 2–6–0 No 46521 passes Northwood Farm with a Santa Special from Arley to Bewdley. This engine of LMS design was built at Swindon in 1953.

11.12.82 Hugh Ballantyne

The foundation stone of the Victoria Bridge being laid. This sketch was drawn by Alexander G. Linn, assistant engineer to the Severn Valley Railway.

December 1859 Author's collection

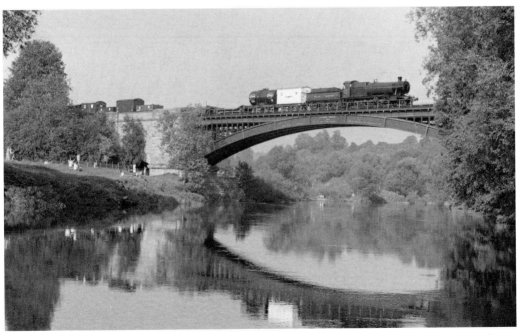

Ex-GWR 28XX class 2–8–0 No. 2857 crosses Victoria Bridge with the 1432 Highley to Bearley, a special goods train run during an Enthusiasts' Weekend.

28.9.85 Hugh Ballantyne

Returned to traffic in 1989, 57XX class 0–6–0PT No. 5784 comes off the Victoria Bridge with a Kidderminster to Bridgnorth train. This picture would have been impossible had not the lineside clearing gang removed excess trees and vegetation.

24.9.89 Hugh Ballantyne

Arley, view towards Bridgnorth. Permanent way wagons are temporarily stabled on the main line.

5.2.94 Author

# Bewdley to Newnham Bridge

The Tenbury Railway opened on 1 August 1861 from Woofferton, on the Shrewsbury and Hereford line, and was extended by the Tenbury, Bewdley, Kidderminster and Worcester Junction Railway to join the Severn Valley Railway at Bewdley, the necessary Act on 3 July 1860 allowing it to raise £120,000 by shares and £40,000 in loans. The line was engineered by John Fowler, assisted by D. Wylie. Later, Fowler was to be the co-designer of the Forth Bridge and consulting engineer for London's first tube railway. The contract for building the line was let to Brassey and Field.

On 5 August 1864 work was sufficiently advanced for the directors and their friends to make a trial trip along the completed line. The Board of Trade inspection took place on 9 August 1864 and public traffic commenced on 13 August. The TBK&WJR was worked by the GWR and vested in that company by an Act of 12 July 1869.

Although passenger traffic was withdrawn from the branch on 1 August 1962, an experimental service was introduced from Tenbury to Bewdley. This weekday morning train and a return in the evening survived until 1 August 1963. General goods traffic ended on 6 January 1964 and the branch closed entirely on 15 April 1965 when there was no more traffic from the Cleobury Mortimer and Dittons Prior Light Railway, which had been owned by the Royal Naval Armaments Depot since 30 September 1957, when it purchased the line from BR to give access to its store.

At the north end of Bewdley Viaduct the Tenbury branch ran parallel with the SVR and a mile north of Bewdley station curved and descended westwards to Dowles Bridge over the River Severn. This structure consisted of three lattice girder deck spans each 70 feet long. Beyond was an ascent to Cleobury Mortimer, with a ruling gradient of 1 in 70. Wyre Forest station consisted of a platform and siding on the Up side of the single track. By 1925 its signal-box was closed and replaced with a ground frame. Just west of the station, the branch, which had closely followed the county boundary, entered Shropshire.

Cleobury Mortimer, just in Shropshire, had a passing loop, while additional sidings were laid to cope with increased traffic brought by the opening of the Dittons Prior branch to goods on 1 July 1908 and to passengers on 19 November. South of Cleobury Mortimer the branch re-entered Worcestershire and just before Neen Stollars crossed the River Rea on a brick bridge.

Neen Stollars, originally with a single platform on the Down side and a goods loop beyond, had its loop extended on 13 July 1924 when a Down platform was added. This feature was taken out of use and the layout simplified with the closure of the signal-box on 22 August 1954.

The line closely followed the bank of the River Rea to Newnham Bridge station, which had a single platform on the Down side of the line. The goods yard was sited east of the passenger station. Fairly early in this century its signal-box was closed and replaced by three ground frames, and a loop added opposite the passenger platform. As access to the latter could only be across the running line, the Working Time Table Appendix stipulated: 'Loading and Unloading of Heavy Goods to and from Road Vehicles at the platform obstructing the running line . . . the practice of backing vehicles to the platform must not be resorted to when it is possible to avoid it'. Traffic sent from the station included fruit and rabbits. About midway to Tenbury the line recrossed into Shropshire.

Early this century passenger trains tended to be worked by Metro class 2–4–0Ts, 517 class 0–4–2Ts and Dean Goods 0–6–0s. In 1931 it was recorded that a Metro tank and a 1661 class 0–6–0PT were at work. From 1941 GWR diesel railcars Nos 19, 25 and 33 were to be seen, together with 45XX 2–6–2Ts. During the Second World War, LNER J25 class 0–6–0s Nos 2059, 2061 and 2142, on loan to the GWR, were sometimes used on the Stourbridge to Hereford goods train. They performed well on the gradient to Cleobury Mortimer, but were very heavy on coal. Collett 0–6–0s and Aberdare 2–6–0s could be seen on Hereford to Stourbridge freights. Kidderminster Co-operative Society chartered trains during the summer for day excursions to various resorts, those to South Wales usually involving a route over the Tenbury branch. The train of ten coaches and a buffet car was handled by a 2–6–0 and 2–6–2T.

The passenger service varied very little over the years in either frequency, or the time taken for a journey from Bewdley to Newnham Bridge, which remained at 35 minutes. In 1887 four trains were scheduled to run each way; in the 1920s it was five and in the summer of 1930, six. During the Second World War the service was reduced to four but increased to five in postwar years. With the opening of the Kidderminster Loop on 1 June 1878 a through service was introduced between Birmingham and Woofferton, as this could now be operated without the need for reversal. This included an LNWR through coach coupled at Smethwick Junction to the GWR train which originated at Birmingham (Snow Hill). This working ceased on 1 January 1917. With the opening of the Kidderminster Loop, the Down direction on the Tenbury branch was reversed, Bewdley to Newnham Bridge becoming Up.

2–4–0WT No. 1A crosses Dowles Bridge with the Board of Trade inspector's train. The barge on the far right was used by the line's contractor, Thomas Brassey.

9.8.1864 Author's collection

Wyre Forest station, view towards Newnham Bridge.

*c.* 1910 Author's collection

131

Ex-GWR diesel railcar W20W rises to approach the Bridgnorth to Stourport line which it will run parallel with to Bewdley. The train is the 3.05 p.m. Tenbury to Kidderminster.

20.6.59 Michael Mensing

57XX class 0–6–0 PT No. Bewdeley with the 3.05 p.m. Tenbury to Kidderminster. Note the quarter mile post in the foreground, the distance from Paddington being via Oxford and Worcester.

15.8.59 Michael Mensing

Wyre Forest station, view towards Bewdley.

*c.* 1910 Author's collection

The very domestic-looking approach to Newnham Bridge station.

*c.* 1960 Lens of Sutton

Ex-GWR diesel railcar W20W receding, as indicated by the tail lamp, from the camera, while working the 4.58 p.m. Tenbury to Hartlebury.

20.6.59 Michael Mensing

An ex-GWR railcar about to leave Newnham Bridge for Bewdley. The crossing in the foreground is made from old sleepers. Notice the fruit vans in the siding on the left.

21.7.56 G. Bannister

Newnham Bridge station.

*c.* 1960 Lens of Sutton

Stanier class 3 2–6–2T No. 40126 approaches Bewdley with the 1.45 p.m. Shrewsbury to Kidderminster. The Tenbury branch is on the right.

25.6.60 Michael Mensing

Ex-GWR diesel railcar W202W calls at Wyre Forest with the 4.10 p.m. Kidderminster to Tenbury. Evidently no problem existed with bicycle conveyance by railcar in 1959!

20.6.59 Michael Mensing

No. 7819 *Hinton Manor* leaves Bewdley Tunnel with the 1118 Kidderminster to Bridgnorth.

24.9.89 Hugh Ballantyne

# Stourbridge Junction to Stourbridge Town

The OWWR Act of 23 July 1858 authorized an inclined railway which left the Stourbridge Junction to Wolverhampton line at Stourbridge Engine House signal-box and descended past the incline's engine house to the canal basin. Construction began in April 1859, the opening ceremony taking place on 30 July the same year, though a locomotive and four horses were used as the winding engine had yet to be installed. This haste was necessary because the Act stipulated that the line must be opened by 31 July 1859. The branch did not open properly for nearly another two years. The incline closed on 1 January 1880, being rendered redundant by a new branch with somewhat easier gradients.

On 5 July 1865 the Stourbridge Railway obtained powers for building the Stourbridge Town branch and the following year an Act of 16 July allowed a deviation of route. No concrete action was taken before 1 February 1870, when the Stourbridge Railway was vested in the GWR. The original powers having lapsed, on 30 June 1874 the GWR obtained an Act for the construction of the line, though work did not begin until the late spring of 1878. It opened for passengers on 1 October 1879 and to goods on 1 January 1880. As mentioned on page 83, the re-siting of Stourbridge Junction station necessitated modifying the main line end of the branch and this was brought into use on 1 October 1901. As a wartime economy measure the branch closed to passengers on 29 March 1915, trains being replaced by GWR buses. The rail passenger service was restored on 3 March 1919, but closed again during the 1926 General Strike, when GWR AEC buses operated a service between 7 May and 10 July. Stourbridge Basin closed to goods on 5 July 1965, the Town closing to goods traffic a few months later on 20 September, but the branch was not singled and the goods line taken out of use until 22 October 1967. At the time of writing the branch is closed from January to April 1994 for the rebuilding of Stourbridge Town station, a replacement bus service being operated.

Less than three-quarters of a mile in length, the branch is BR's shortest; the change at Stourbridge Junction is irritating and to some extent time-wasting. From 27 August 1935 the double track was converted to one passenger and one goods line, the Up line becoming Up and Down goods. Each line was worked with a wooden train staff under the 'one engine in steam' system, this economy of having two parallel single lines enabling Stourbridge Town signal-box to be closed on 27 August 1935.

From the junction the branch falls at 1 in 67 and during the last decade at least two DMUs have run through the buffers into the bus station. Stourbridge Town had a largish, light-coloured brick-built passenger station decorated with red brick and stone sills and lintels. It was situated on the Down side of the line. In 1931 Passimeter equipment was installed at a cost of £204, the turnstile allowing the booking clerk to control access to and from the platform and obviating the need for a ticket collector. The station lost its platform canopy in the 1970s. On 18 February 1979 a new 57 yard-long platform was opened 52 yards nearer Stourbridge Junction, the old station site becoming part of the enlarged bus station. The new platform, with a bus shelter as a waiting room, was Stand L of the bus station.

The station was the railhead for the GWR bus service to Hagley and Belbroughton, which commenced on 13 February 1905 using Milnes-Daimler double-deckers. Later the route was extended to Catshill and Bromsgrove, the service being withdrawn on 5 August 1916.

Beyond the passenger station the single-track goods line descended at 1 in 27 and the Operating Appendix ruled: 'In all cases guards working Up or Down branch trains must ride outside their van compartment at the hand brake in readiness to give instant attention'. The line crossed the River Stour and curved round past the gasworks to the basin of the Stourbridge Canal. Here were two goods sheds, a transit shed, and goods and private sidings. The line re-crossed the River Stour to the ironworks of Messrs Bradley and Company. Until the track was lifted, the rails at Lower High Street bore grooves where the 3 ft 6 in gauge Dudley, Stourbridge and District Electric Traction Company Limited's tramway crossed.

Steam railmotors were introduced to the branch in January 1905 and worked it for over thirty years. In fact it was one of their last haunts and they made almost sixty trips daily until October 1935. The interior of a railmotor was gas-lit, the exterior head lamp supplied by the Locomotive Department and the tail lamp by the Carriage Department. As well as the saloons being well-cleaned daily at Stourbridge locomotive depot, the station-master arranged for them to be swept out and kept 'thoroughly clean' during the day. Less than six months after the cessation of the steam railmotors, diesel railcars made their appearance. First was No. 8 in March 1936, followed by No. 14 and No. 15. Also used were 14XX class 0–4–2Ts, or 64XX 0–6–0PTs, hauling an auto trailer, including *Wren* built by BR in 1951. As the branch had no intermediate station, it was one of the few where passenger trains were allowed to work without a guard. In 1958 BR DMUs arrived. Goods trains were worked by 57XX class 0–6–0PTs.

The line enjoyed an initial train service of seventeen trains each way taking 3 minutes. By August 1887 the branch had eleven Down and ten Up, no Sunday service being worked. By April 1910 fity-three trains were run each way on weekdays and seventeen on Sundays. The latter were withdrawn during the First World War and never restored. In July 1922 there were forty-six trains each way, while in July 1938 the service showed sixty-nine Down and sixty-six Up trains. This had decreased to fifty-eight and fifty-two respectively by 1960. The current service is more frequent than ever, with seventy-eight each way appearing in the 1993–4 timetable. The time taken is still 3 minutes.

Mercifully the branch has been free from serious accidents, but on 17 July 1936 a collision at Stourbridge Junction between a goods and an auto train resulted in the death of the auto train driver and injury to one passenger.

OWWR engine 'A' which hauled the first train from Stourbridge to Evesham on 1 May 1852

An auto car, pushed from Stourbridge Town by 14XX class 0–4–2T No. 1438, approaches
Stourbridge Junction. It is crossing from the former Down line, as, from 1935, passenger trains in
both directions used the Down line and all goods trains the Up line.

*c.* 1954 M.E.J. Deane

Photograph taken from about the same viewpoint forty years later. In the distance Sprinter 150 120
prepares to reverse to form the 1257 to Birmingham (New Street).

5.2.94 Author

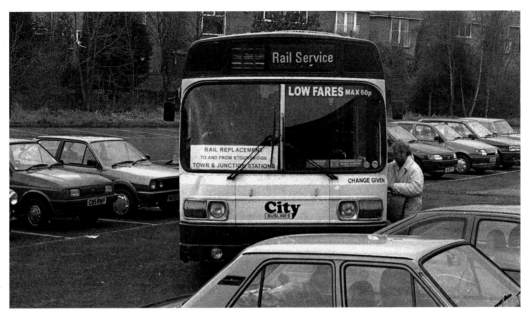

The rail replacement bus service from Stourbridge Town takes on a passenger at the Junction. Notices read: 'Low Fares Max 60p', 'Rail Replacement to and from Stourbridge Town & Junction Stations'.

5.2.94 Author

The attractively painted overbridges near Stourbridge Junction station. The Town branch is in the foreground, with the main line beyond. The BR/Centro sign makes the drive to Stourbridge Junction station.

5.2.94

Gloucester Railway Carriage and Wagon Company motor brake second single-unit DMU W55006 south of Stourbridge Town with the 2.58 p.m. ex-Stourbridge Junction.

11.6.62 Michael Mensing

Gloucester Railway Carriage and Wagon Company motor brake second single-unit DMU W55006 leaving Stourbridge Town with the 3.40 p.m. to Stourbridge Junction.

11.6.62 Michael Mensing

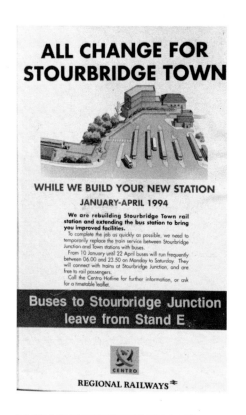

Poster showing sketch of the new station at Stourbridge Town and details of closure and replacement bus service.

5.2.94. Author

Gloucester Railway Carriage and Wagon Company motor brake second M55012 at Stourbridge Town with the 1845 ex-Stourbridge Junction.

17.6.78 Michael Mensing

Temporary ticket office at Stourbridge Town used during the station rebuilding.

5.2.94 Author

14XX class 0–4–2T No. 1438 (84F Stourbridge Junction) at Stourbridge Town with an auto coach. The goods line is on the left.

*c*. 1954 M.E.J. Deane

Contractors' plant for building the new Stourbridge Town station.

5.2.94 Author

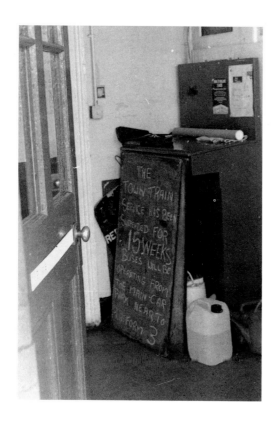

The blackboard in an office at Stourbridge Junction station announces: 'The Town train service has been suspended for 15 weeks. Buses will be operating from the main car park near to Platform 3'.

5.2.94 Author